Visual Finance

This page intentionally left blank.

Visual

Finance

THE ONE PAGE VISUAL
MODEL TO UNDERSTAND
FINANCIAL STATEMENTS
AND MAKE BETTER DECISIONS

Georgi Tsvetanov

This publication is designed to provide accurate and authoritative information about the subject matter covered. It is sold with the understanding that the publisher and author are not engaged in rendering legal, accounting, or other professional services. If legal advice or other expert assistance is required, the services of a competent professional person should be sought.

ISBN 978-1518647451

To my wife Carolina who supported me unconditionally.
To my son Vladimir who was my inspiration to finish this book. I love you both.

This page intentionally left blank.

Table of Contents

This page intentionally left blank.

Introduction

This page intentionally left blank.

Do you speak the language of business?

The language of business is English

Finance

Think of a financial decision you recently made: investing in new equipment, changing your insurance provider, opening a savings account, applying for credit - you name it.

Chances are, you analyzed different options to ensure your choice was the best fit for your needs. Recent economic studies, however, show that people lack the knowledge and skills to make intelligent financial decisions. Only 46% of respondents demonstrated an average or higher level of financial literacy.

Economic knowledge is essential both on a personal and professional level. Managing your family finances wisely helps you prepare for hard times and retirement. Making better business decisions as an employee boosts your career and can lead to promotion. As a business owner, financial literacy helps you be more successful and grow your business more quickly.

Accounting is the language of business. Some people such as accountants and CFOs are fluent in this language. However, those without a financial background often struggle to understand that language, and miss opportunities to make timely, appropriate decisions.

In the same way that learning a foreign language opens your mind to new ways of thinking, learning the financial language teaches you new ways of looking at business.

Businesses measure performance in numbers: sales, growth, ROI, ROE, delivery time, and employees' commitment. The logic of accounting is virtually the same in every country. After finishing this book, you will be able to understand financial statements even when they're in a language you don't know, such as Mandarin, German, or Russian.

Accounting is a way of measuring, analyzing, and communicating financial information about a business. It is one of the most exciting business fields. If you are not convinced yet, hopefully by the time you finish reading this book you will be! The way a company manages its assets, cash flow, and costs can mean the difference between success and failure.

Revenue	100
売上原価	40
Gemeinkosten	30
Налоги	10
صافي الربح	20

What you will learn

This book is for anyone who wants to:

Understand the story numbers are telling.
The company is a complex system that continually evolves.
Business acumen will help you understand what is happening.

Recognize trends and warning signals long before problems occur.

Improve your judgment by better understanding the financial
impact of your choices.

Understand the connections.
A decision that the sales department makes might affect
operations in an unexpected way. Business acumen will help you
explore such relationships and minimize potential conflicts.

Who this book is for?

Entrepreneur
Grow your business and be even more successful

Do you already have a business, or plan to start or acquire one?
The Visual Finance model will help you better understand numbers,
understand the changing market reality, measure the value of your
company, and compare your company with the competition.

Employee
Stand up to your CFO

Speaking the language of top management will enhance your
credibility and provide opportunities for career growth. You will also
understand the relationships between different areas of your
company and be able to align your efforts with organizational
objectives.

Student
Impress your accounting professor

If you are a student, this book will help you understand accounting and business finance quickly and in a more interactive way.

Investor
Compare different investment opportunities

If you're an investor, this book will help you read financial statements more insightfully, and highlight additional information you can take from them. In a dedicated chapter, we will also discuss how to analyze the credibility of those financial statements.

Your role within the company

Different roles within a company have different needs.

Businesses want to sell more, innovate, and have motivated employees, but executives feel the pressure to reduce costs, work smarter, and deal with tough competition from all over the world.

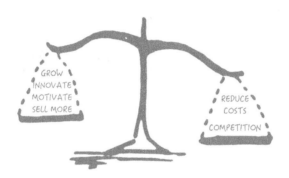

BY THEIR VERY NATURE FINANCIAL ANALYSTS TEND TO BE DEFENSIVE, CONSERVATIVE, AND PESSIMISTIC. ON THE OTHER SIDE GUYS IN SALES AND MARKETING ARE AGGRESSIVE, SPECULATIVE, AND OPTIMISTIC. THEY'RE SAYING LET'S DO IT, WHILE THE BEAN COUNTERS ARE CAUTIONING WHY YOU SHOULDN'T. [...]

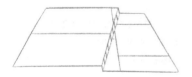

IF THE BEAN COUNTERS ARE TOO WEAK, THE COMPANY WILL SPEND ITSELF INTO BANKRUPTCY. BUT, IF THEY ARE TOO STRONG THE COMPANY WOULD NOT MEET THE MARKET OR STAY COMPETITIVE. IN A COMPANY YOU NEED BOTH SIDES OF THE EQUATION.

- Lee Iacocca, Autobiography

If you are in marketing, sales, or R&D, you will learn how to express your goals numerically, make them more realistic, and determine how they might impact other areas.

If you belong to the "bean counters" (meaning you work in finance or accounting), you will learn how to contribute to the big picture and what pressures the other areas are experiencing.

Here are specific benefits you can gain from deepening your financial knowledge, broken down by work area:

CEO

Find new ways to meet investors' expectations. Enhance your understanding of what impacts the stock price of your company and why.

Finance and Accounting

Explore a new way to look at corporate finance and a new instructional tool to help you explain it more clearly to your colleagues.

Human Resources and Training

Increase your credibility by more accurately estimating the ROI of different initiatives.

Marketing, Sales

Demonstrate the benefits of your products or services in a measurable and credible way. This book will be exceptionally helpful if you sell large ticket business-to-business solutions and need to prove ROI. You will also be able to detect more missing opportunities and predict revenue more accurately.

IT

Correctly measure the cost and return of major technological investments.

Manufacturing and Operations

Understand what affects costs and how to keep up with production goals. Examine efficiency of processes and utilization of assets, and improve inventory management.

R&D and Engineering

Develop your ability to get profitable products to market on time and control ever-growing design costs.

If you are an HR manager, trainer or a university professor, then the model presented in this book will help you teach finance in a more interactive way.

Imagine having 100% instead of 46% of employees think like owners and implement new ways to improve efficiency, profitability, and liquidity.

If you want to take your educational method to the next level, we recommend you use the Silega Pulse ™business simulation developed and sold by Silega.

Please contact global@silega.com or visit silega.com for more details.

Why Visual Finance?

In a recent study, only 46% of respondents had average or higher financial literacy and could understand financial reports.

Non-financial executives are less than enthusiastic about accounting. This could partly be in reaction to the way business schools teach it. Accounting is perceived as tedious, complicated, and too theoretical.

Stop avoiding financial topics during team meetings. Save your company from making costly mistakes and start maximizing all the valuable opportunities.

Visual Finance is a powerful, simple tool that you can learn in just a couple of hours and easily apply to real life. Over the past five years, this model has been used in thousands of "finance for non-financial managers" training sessions in more than 30 countries.

Now, for the first time, it has finally been released in a paperback format.

Accounting is easier than you think

Three common myths that create resistance towards numbers:

Accounting requires good mathematical skills.

False! You can always use software and calculators to do the math. Accounting is a way of thinking and understanding the logic behind a business. Plus, you may notice that in this book numbers are almost absent until the last part.

Learning accounting is time-consuming and requires reading thick, annoying books.

False! To understand the fundamental concepts behind financial reports, you will need less than four hours.

My company already has accountants; I don't need to invest my time and effort.

Another version of this is "I'm a business owner, and I can always hire an accounting firm."

False! Studying accounting gives you a much broader understanding of business. Moreover, numbers you're currently dealing with may not be even valid. Even if you're a non-financial executive, your performance is inevitably measured in numbers. If those numbers align with your company's global priorities, your value will increase.

Frequently asked questions

This book is written following a particular flow of logic. Reading it as structured will help you better understand the ideas behind the one-page model. However, you might be looking for the answer to a particular question. Here are some of the most frequently asked questions about accounting:

What type of accounting?

Accounting is the system of recording, measuring and communicating financial information.

There are different types of accounting, including financial and managerial accounting. Both are necessary for a business, but they serve different purposes.

Managerial accounting, as its name suggests, is used mainly by management to make estimates. This type of account points to the future. Financial accounting, on the other hand, serves stakeholders such as government, owners, and creditors. The purpose is to give an accurate report of the company's past performance.

The chart below shows the differences and similarities between managerial and financial accounting:

	Managerial accounting	Financial accounting
Users	Internal users (usually management)	External users such as creditors, investors, government
Purpose	Planning and control	Credit and investment decisions
Input	Future estimations, plans, historical data	Past transactions
Output	Budgets and reports	Financial reports: Income statements (P&L), balance sheets, cash flow statements, etc.
Frequency	As needed	Quarterly and annually
Flexibility	Allowed	Defined by standards (such as GAAP) and verified by auditors

This page intentionally left blank.

How companies create value?

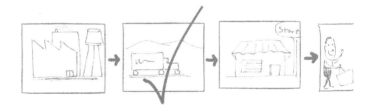

This page intentionally left blank.

Why is your company in business?

What makes a company successful? Make a list of factors that would be true for businesses of any size, from large multi-national corporations to small, family-run establishments.

Your list probably includes cash, people, products, innovation, profit, sustainability, innovation, and investors.

Now rearrange your list in order of importance, and narrow it down to the single most important factor.

Defining Value

Profit

If you wrote profit, you're right! Business is a repetitive process that creates earnings for owners by delivering a product or service to clients.
The opposite of being profitable is losing money and going out of business.

No profit for a sustained period = bankruptcy

The other success factors are all valid responses. However, even a company with the best people or product will eventually fail to deliver on its promise if it is not profitable.
As Stephen Covey says, "No Margin, No Mission".

Cash

Cash and profit are two different things. Even a profitable business can run out of money, which will inevitably halt all operations.
Without cash, the company will not be able to pay its employees, providers, and creditors.

No cash = a business standstills

Sustainability

Picture a profitable company where management exchanges long-term vision for short-term gains and makes ethically questionable decisions. When such practices are exposed, scandals erupt, businesses are ruined, and some people even end up in prison. Infamous examples include Enron, Tyco International, Sunbeam, and Parmalat.

Lack of sustainability = vulnerability

Growth

Business success depends on the ability to innovate, change, and grow. Without this flexibility, a company cannot respond to changing customer preferences or dynamic competition. Organizations that lost their edge and stopped growing and changing include Eastman Kodak, Blockbuster, Motorola, Sears, Sony, and Yahoo.

Lack of growth = inability to meet changing customer preferences or competition

Economic value is created by being profitable, managing cash wisely, acting sustainability, and continuing to grow.

Those are the factors owners and investors constantly monitor as the vital signs of a company's health.

THE COMPANY

Creating Value

Making money is critical, but is not the single reason for a business to exist. The fact that we survive by eating does not mean we live to eat. To be profitable, growing, sustainable, and solvent, companies must serve a larger purpose.

How exactly does your organization create value? Please list at least three examples from your experience of how your product or service is valuable.

Your examples probably fall into one or few of the following categories:

Constant innovation

"Only we have it!"

Your company aims at developing a technological superiority over the competition.

Superior quality

"We offer the best product or service!"

Quality leads to fewer complaints and lower repair costs, and guarantees customer satisfaction.

Exceptional customer service

"No one treats you like we do!"

You strive to anticipate and satisfy customer needs.

Faster or Cheaper

"We guarantee you cannot find it cheaper or faster!"

You offer guaranteed delivery and lower prices than the competition.

younique

Unique design

"How cool is this."

You differentiate yourself from other products with similar features.

Customization

"Have it your way!"

You understand customers better than anyone else and deliver exactly what they need.

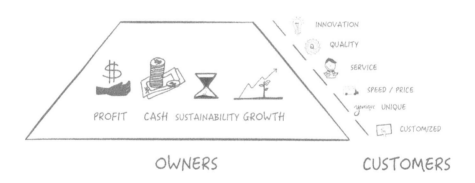

OWNERS

PROFIT   CASH   SUSTAINABILITY   GROWTH

INNOVATION
QUALITY
SERVICE
SPEED / PRICE
UNIQUE
CUSTOMIZED

CUSTOMERS

Maximizing Value

Value means different things to the different people involved.

For management, value is about maximizing activities that create a positive return and minimizing unproductive ones.

For owners, value implies that the corporation is profitable and returns are worth the investment.

For employees, a good company provides competitive pay and a sense of purpose.

For providers, working with a stable company guarantees increased sales.

For customers, value is getting the best product or service at a competitive price.

If a company is successful, the value it creates spreads to the whole market:
- It hires more people and pays better;
- It orders more goods from providers;
- It shares more dividends with investors;
- It pays more taxes, thereby injecting money into the economy.

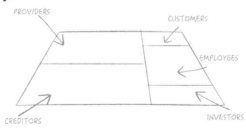

Business as a movement

Each business is a value creation process. It starts with an input and ends with a finished product or service.

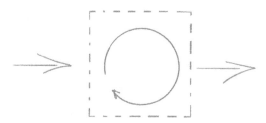

A company producing a good or service buys raw material, adds value in the process, sells the end product through its distribution channels, and charges for all those factors. That model is accurate for the automotive, food and beverages, agriculture, pharmaceuticals, construction, energy, and transportation industries.

Some businesses do not produce a tangible product; the value is created by the people rather than by transforming physical raw materials. This applies to industries such as consulting, media, entertainment, and education.

Below you can find some examples:

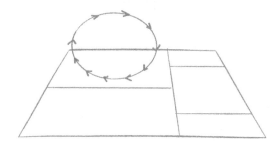

Banking, financial

The raw material for the banking industry is money that depositors place in accounts.

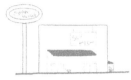

Retail

In the retail business, companies sell a product or service produced by someone else. In this case, they add value by organizing their supply chain to reach more customers in a more efficient way.

The progression is like this: provider (manufacturer) to wholesaler/distribution center to sales floor.
A company might distribute a tangible product (food, equipment) or provide a service (travel agency).

Government

Instead of generating revenue, government entities have an assigned budget and create value by performing a particular service or delivering a product.

Business	Input	Value generation process	Output
MANUFACTURING Automotive Pharmaceuticals Chemicals Engineering Food and beverages	Raw materials	Value through design and assembly	Finished goods
RETAIL Wholesale Online sales	Goods from suppliers	Distribution, making goods available in locations closer to customers	Goods delivered to end customer
INFRASTRUCTURE, UTILITIES Hotels Airlines	Assets (property, infrastructure, machinery)	Usage of assets	Service
PEOPLE SERVICES Consulting Software Auditing	People's knowledge and experience.	Generate solutions that are beneficial to customers	New product development, new service
FINANCE Banking Insurance	Customer's money	Loan money with interest; accept cash for interest	Financial service (savings, credit)

Resources for creating value:

The balance sheet

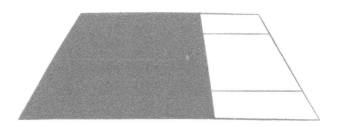

This page intentionally left blank.

What do you have, and what do you owe?

So far we've examined the importance of having a business that is profitable, growing, and sustainable. We've also explored how a company creates value.

What resources can a business use to deliver on this promise and execute its strategy? Write them down:

Here are some resources you might have listed:
Property
Cash
Machinery, equipment
Inventory

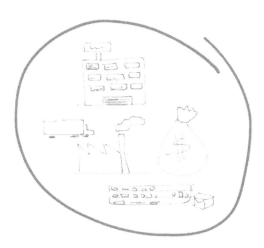

All the resources that your company possesses are assets. They have several things in common:

1. Assets have a positive financial value; in other words, you can convert them into cash by selling them (cash is also an asset).

2. Assets are completely controlled by and can be disposed of by your company.

3. Assets are currently used (and will be used in the future) to produce a product or service.

We'll use the following visual symbol for assets, because they are designed to be continuously used to generate value for business owners.

Now that we've listed what a business has, let's consider how those resources were obtained. Write down some suggestions:

Everything that a company has (its assets) was generated over time using two sources of funding:

Owners (investors). This includes money that partners funded into the business either directly or by reinvesting profit rather than withdrawing it. This is called owner's equity.

Banks (creditors). Companies also borrow money from financial institutions to be able to grow more quickly and aggressively. This is called liability.

Those are the two primary sources of funding for an enterprise. In other words, everything that you own (i.e., assets) is either funded by creditors or owners (investors).

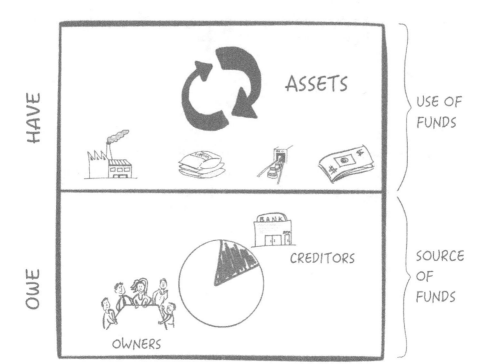

Two types of debt

Current liabilities or short-term liabilities are all those obligations that should be settled in less than a year such as payments to providers. The objective of short-term debt is to ensure that the business has enough cash to continue operating and minimize the risk of running out of cash. Current liabilities cover short-term financing needs.

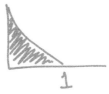

Long-term debt (also known as fixed liability) is usually paid in more than one year. This typically includes long-term bank loans or mortgage loans that have payback periods of up to twenty or more years. Long term liability is used to purchase major assets such as equipment and property.

Long-term debt provides several advantages for business:
-   Growth opportunities. With liability, a business can grow more quickly and acquire significant assets (i.e., a new factory, or even a competitor).
-   Increased stability through lower interest rates. Long-term debt conditions usually have a lower cost and are structured in regular fixed payments (ergo, fixed liability).

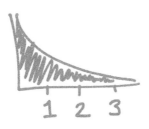

Two type of assets

Here are some of the assets a company usually possesses:

- Cash: money in bank accounts

- Accounts receivable: cash customers owe the company (it belongs to the firm; however, it is not available until customers pay)

- Inventory: raw material, product in process, and finished goods

- Property: real estate and buildings

- Machinery and equipment

Some assets are better when they are moving. The more sales you have, the more inventory you move. The more inventory you move, the more receivables and cash you will have.

Cash, accounts receivable, and inventory are also known as current assets. They convert quickly into cash, and are expected to be sold or used during a typical business cycle. Current assets are meant to be in motion, and the more you move them, the better for the business.

Other assets are meant to be moved infrequently or not at all. Assets such as property, facilities, vehicles, furniture, and equipment are called long-term assets or fixed assets. These are used to produce value. However, they are not the product sold directly to the customer. (Unless your company constructs and sells buildings or industrial equipment.)

Of course, a corporation in need could sell its fixed assets, but this could damage the company's production capacity and would require valuable time for the deal to be settled.

Introducing the balance sheet

The financial statement that shows what a corporation owns and owes is called balanced sheet.
The chart below shows assets (what you have) on the left side and obligations (liability and owner's equity) on the right side.

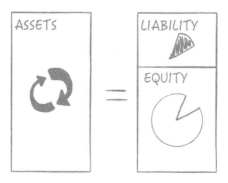

Another and a more common way to show the balance sheet is placing assets on top followed by liability and equity.

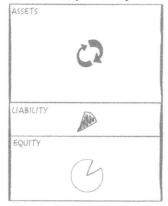

However, the first figure better shows the logic behind the balance sheet, that the assets should equal the liability plus the equity. But why? Is this always true? Let's examine some compelling cases.

Your personal balance sheet

Let's analyze your particular financial situation, where the same logic applies. You have assets, i.e., things you own that have monetary value. If you decide to, you can sell them and convert them into cash. Assets include things such as your savings, car, house, household appliances, money lent to friends, etc.

Make a list of all your assets:

Although it would take time, it's possible to quantify the total value of all your assets.

Let's imagine that the value of all your assets is $300,000.

You'll probably also have some debt, such as mortgage payments and bank loans. Suppose that the amount of your debt equals $100,000.

In this case, your personal equity (called net worth) is the difference of $200,000.

The balance sheet is always "balanced"; everything that you have (assets) is either financed by debt (i.e. credit) or belongs to you (equity).

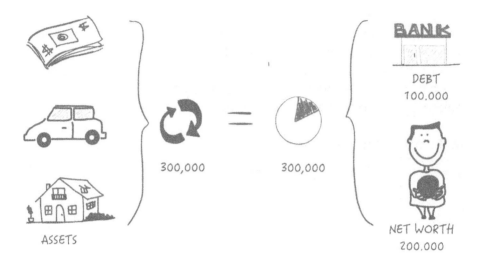

ASSETS 300,000 = 300,000

BANK

DEBT
100.000

NET WORTH
200.000

A company's balance sheet

The same logic applies to a company's balance sheet. Everything that the business owns (assets) was either funded by the owners (initial investment and retained earnings) or the creditors.

The parts of the balance sheet always move in tandem. If one side increases or decreases, so does the other. Let's examine some scenarios.

If a business borrows money from a bank, the enterprise will have more cash available. The left side will increase because the cash is an asset. However, the right side will also rise. The company will owe this money, therefore it represents a liability.

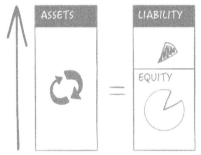

In a different scenario, if the same organization pays back part of its debt in cash, liabilities will decrease, and so will assets.

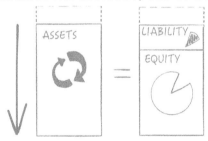

Where does the profit go?

After a successful year, management decides to keep the profit within the company instead of paying dividends. In such cases, both sides of the balance sheet will increase. The company will have more assets on the left, and more equity on the right.

What happens if the opposite occurs and the company suffers a loss?

On the right side of the equation, there are two sorts of obligations: liability and equity. The bank has the right to demand its money back, just as the owners have the right to claim their share.

Yet there is a fundamental difference. Credit is a non-negotiable obligation. Banks minimize their risk; they lend money at a specific interest rate. If their client is doing well, financial institutions are not entitled to share the profit and can only claim the appropriate interest. If their client performs poorly and experiences loss, banks still have the right to demand the money borrowed.

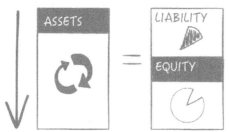

On the other hand, owner's equity is not guaranteed. Investors carry all the risk. If the business is thriving, their money increases. However, if there is a loss, partners will take a big blow and their wealth will decrease, sometimes even to the point of lost ownership or negative equity.

Not all movements in the balance sheet involve both sides. Sometimes one type of asset is converted to another type without changing the debt of the company.

Consider the following examples:
- Charging a customer (converting accounts receivables to cash)
- Using cash to purchase raw materials
- Selling a piece of equipment for cash

In all those cases, the total value of assets will still be the same.

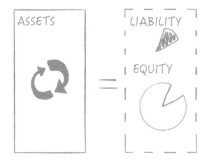

Abstract:

The left side of the one page model represents the balance sheet, showing:
a) what the company has
b) how and by whom it was funded: what part of its capital is borrowed from financial institutions and what part is backed by the owners (shareholders)

For further reference, we will use the " ↻ " Symbol for assets,

and the " ◔ " symbol for obligations towards creditors and owners.

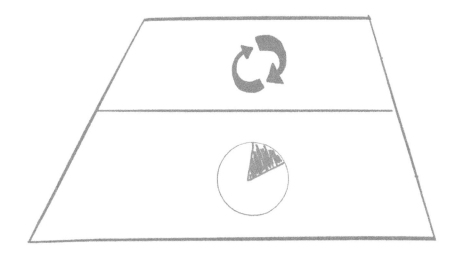

Application: examining a sample balance sheet

Let's analyze the balance sheet of a real company. Take General Electric Company (NYSE:GE) for instance. You can access the balance sheet for any public company directly from their website or from web portals such as Yahoo Finance. Go to https://www.finance.yahoo.com. In the "Quote lookup" box, type "GE," then from the "Financials" menu, select "Balance Sheet."

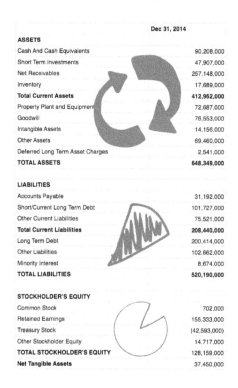

	Dec 31, 2014
ASSETS	
Cash And Cash Equivalents	90,208,000
Short Term Investments	47,907,000
Net Receivables	257,148,000
Inventory	17,689,000
Total Current Assets	**412,952,000**
Property Plant and Equipment	72,687,000
Goodwill	76,553,000
Intangible Assets	14,156,000
Other Assets	69,460,000
Deferred Long Term Asset Charges	2,541,000
TOTAL ASSETS	**648,349,000**
LIABILITIES	
Accounts Payable	31,192,000
Short/Current Long Term Debt	101,727,000
Other Current Liabilities	75,521,000
Total Current Liabilities	**208,440,000**
Long Term Debt	200,414,000
Other Liabilities	102,662,000
Minority Interest	8,674,000
TOTAL LIABILITIES	**520,190,000**
STOCKHOLDER'S EQUITY	
Common Stock	702,000
Retained Earnings	155,333,000
Treasury Stock	(42,593,000)
Other Stockholder Equity	14,717,000
TOTAL STOCKHOLDER'S EQUITY	**128,159,000**
Net Tangible Assets	**37,450,000**

What information can we obtain from this document?

First, you will notice that it contains several fiscal periods. (In my example, the latest is 2014.)

Second, let's draw the main three components: assets, liabilities, and equity.

We will split the balance sheet into two to study its logic better.

According to the information above, as of Dec. 2014, General Electric has assets that are valued at $648,349,000. The company uses those assets to produce value for shareholders.

But how did General Electric finance those assets?

The total liabilities of this enterprise are $520,190,000. This represents 80% of assets. So in a way, General Electric is financing its assets with 80% debt. The remaining 20% ($128,159,000) is funded by the stockholders.

And of course, the total amount of the assets equals the liabilities plus the equity as illustrated.

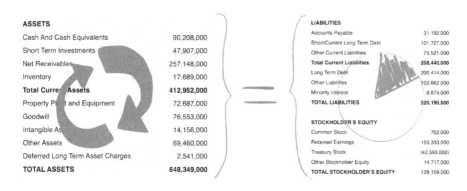

ASSETS		LIABILITIES	
Cash And Cash Equivalents	90,208,000	Accounts Payable	31,192,000
Short Term Investments	47,907,000	Short/Current Long Term Debt	101,727,000
Net Receivables	257,148,000	Other Current Liabilities	75,521,000
Inventory	17,689,000	Total Current Liabilities	208,440,000
Total Current Assets	412,952,000	Long Term Debt	200,414,000
Property Plant and Equipment	72,687,000	Other Liabilities	102,662,000
Goodwill	76,553,000	Minority Interest	8,674,000
Intangible Assets	14,156,000	TOTAL LIABILITIES	520,190,000
Other Assets	69,460,000		
Deferred Long Term Asset Charges	2,541,000	STOCKHOLDER'S EQUITY	
TOTAL ASSETS	648,349,000	Common Stock	702,000
		Retained Earnings	155,333,000
		Treasury Stock	(42,593,000)
		Other Stockholder Equity	14,717,000
		TOTAL STOCKHOLDER'S EQUITY	128,159,000

Take a closer look at the assets.

The *current assets* of General Electric are $412,952,000. Those include:

- Cash and cash equivalents ($90,208,000). Those are the most liquid assets. Cash includes all the money General Electric has in its bank accounts right now (with all currencies converted to USD). Liquid assets such as various securities and treasury bills are readily converted into cash.

- Short-term investments ($47,907,000). Keeping cash in a bank account does not always produce the best return. Businesses keep the excess cash in stocks and bonds. Such investments expire in less than a year and can also be converted into cash.

- Net receivables ($257,148,000). These are also known as accounts receivable, and measure sales delivered to customers but not yet charged.

- Inventory ($17,689,000). This includes all the goods that the company will eventually sell, including raw materials, work in process, and finished goods.

Now, let's take a look at the long-term assets.

- Property, plant and equipment or PP&E. Also known as fixed assets, these are the assets that General Electric uses to produce goods or services. According to the balance sheet, $72,687,000 is the accumulative value of all land, buildings, machinery, vehicles, computers, office equipment, and furniture.

The following two items are both *intangible*, which means they don't have a physical substance.

- Goodwill ($76,553,000). To grow, a company may acquire other businesses and pay more than the market cost. The excess payment is called goodwill. Goodwill is an intangible asset and usually cannot be sold separately; it does not exist on its own outside the business. Examples include the brand, experience on the market, and reputation. Goodwill exists as long as the company exists, and it has an unlimited lifespan.

- Intangible assets ($14,156,000). Such intangibles can exist as separate units and can be sold, bought, or rented. Examples include licenses, copyrights, patents, and franchises. These have a limited lifespan. For example, a copyright will expire after a certain number of years.

- Other assets ($69,460,000). This includes minor assets that do not fit in the previous categories, such as obsolete equipment.

- Deferred long-term asset charges ($2,541,000). This is the value of prepaid expenses, which are an asset because once a company prepays for a service, it has the legal right to claim it.

Next, let's examine the liabilities and the equity.

- Current liabilities ($208,440,000) are all obligations due in less than twelve months. This includes money owed to suppliers (accounts payable), the portion of the long-term debt that the business needs to pay in this accounting period, and other similar charges.

- The long term debt of General Electric ($200,414,000) is all the loans, stocks, and notes issued to obtain funds.

- Other liabilities ($102,662,000) covers debt that does not belong to the former strategic category but is valid for more than twelve months. Estimated future taxes and advanced payments from customers are usually included here.

- Minority interest ($8,674,000) is the value of General Electric's subsidiaries that are not owned by the parent company.

- Common stock, also known as ordinary shares ($702,000), is the part of equity that belongs to common stockholders.

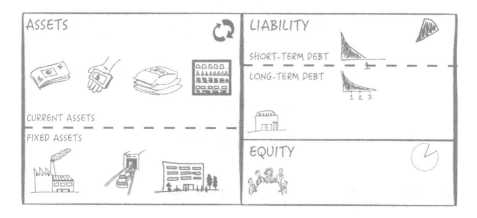

This page intentionally left blank.

What value are you creating?
The income statement

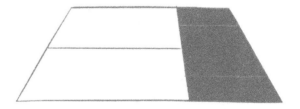

This page intentionally left blank.

How are you doing?

Now let's take a look at the right side of the one page model. This side gives us an entirely new perspective. It tells us how the company is performing – how the business is doing.

We've already discussed value creation. In a business, sales are what creates value, so this column represents the value of sales.

In order to produce and deliver those sales, the company incurs certain expenses such as salaries, raw materials, sales and marketing, and taxes, to name a few.

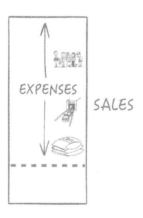

The money that's left after expenses is the profit the business generated during the period (a year or a quarter).

The different types of expenses are as follows:

- Production costs include everything that a business has to spend directly to produce a sale. In the case of a restaurant, those would include the meat, grains, fruit, vegetables, seasonings, and oil used to prepare the food for sale. Production costs are also known as cost of revenue, cost of sale, cost of goods sold (COGS) for production companies, or cost of service (COS) for service companies.

- Salaries (sometimes known as administrative costs) are the price of having your employees working for the company.

- Marketing and sales is the expense of attracting and retaining customers.

- Research and development is the cost of designing new goods.

- Depreciation is the cost of using a company's assets, such as equipment.

- Interest is the cost of borrowing a creditor's money

- Taxes are charges imposed by the state that the company must pay to legally operate in that territory.

Top line to bottom line

The income statement is known by many different names: profit and loss statement (P&L), statement of operations, revenue statement, earning statement, and statement of financial performance. Whatever name you use, this is one of the three financial statements included in the annual public company report. An income statement measures how a business is doing: what value it generates (sales), what value it consumes (expenses), and the value left at the end (profit).

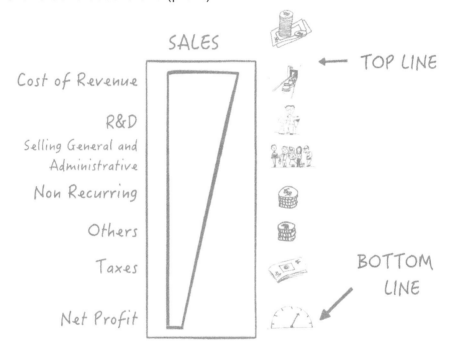

In different terminology, revenue is also known as top line while profit is the bottom line. Improving the top line means selling more, and growing the bottom line means enhancing profit.

Application: examining a sample income statement

Let's review Microsoft's (NASDAQ:MSFT) income statement for 2015, available at the company's website or at Yahoo Finance.

	Jun 30, 2015
Total Revenue	**93,580,000**
Cost of Revenue	33,038,000
Gross Profit	60,542,000
Operating Expenses	
Research Development	12,046,000
Selling General and Administrative	20,324,000
Non Recurring	10,011,000
Operating Income or Loss	**18,161,000**
Total Other Income	346,000
Earnings Before Interest And Taxes	**18,507,000**
Income Tax Expense	6,314,000
NET INCOME (Net Profit)	**12,193,000**

Let's copy the numbers from this Income Statement and paste them into the Visual Finance model:

Sales	93,580,000
Cost of Revenue	33.038.000
R&D	12.046.000
Selling General and Administrative	20.324.000
Non Recurring	10.011.000
Others	346,000
Taxes	6,314,000
Net Profit	12,193,000

Out of the three main financial statements (income statement, balance sheet, and cash flow statement), the income statement is often considered the most practical.

It can be used to make decisions from more practical point of view. While the balance sheet is usually generated for the entire business, income statements can be generated for the whole company or for a single product, factory, or country.

Just by looking at an income statement, you can obtain valuable information about a company's performance.

Sales (revenue)

Every time a corporation delivers a product or a service, it is exchanged for cash or cash claims (accounts receivable).

Revenue is one of the main key performance indicators (KPI) that most senior executive watch closely, no matter the industry. A majority of the CEOs surveyed by the Strategy and Business Development Review says that their critical development activities focus on sales and marketing development.

In a company report, sales can include income sources other than delivering a product or a service, such as royalties or interest from investments.

An interesting conclusion can be drawn by comparing the sales volume of companies competing within the same industry.

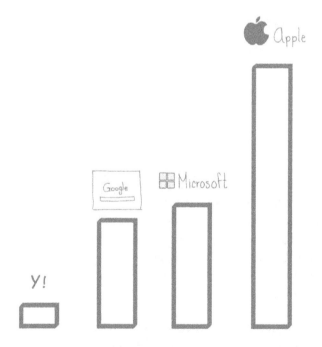

Sales results for 2014: Google (Alphabet Inc, GOOG) 66,001,000; Microsoft (MSFT) 86,833,000; Apple (AAPL) 182,795,000; Yahoo (YHOO) 4,618,133

When is a sale recognized?

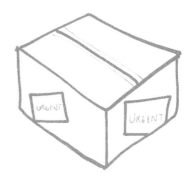

This question can cause controversy, especially if you work for the sales department or if you own a family business.

To some people it seems logical that revenue is recognized only after a customer pays. However, this is wrong.

Sales are recorded when they are earned, which is when a service or product has been delivered. Charging the customer comes afterward.

Sale of tangible goods is recognized on the date of delivery. Revenue from a service is usually recognized at the time of completion. In a case of long-term contracts, a percentage of the sale might be recognized after each stage of the project is delivered.

A sale is not converted into funds automatically. Some companies quickly turn revenue into cash – retail stores, for example. However, for large-ticket sales or business-to-business transactions, this might take months, sometimes even years.

Depreciation: the cost that takes no cash

There are two type of charges: recurring and non-recurring.
Recurring charges include salaries, cost of goods sold, and
marketing. Each business cycle involves moving inventory, paying
employees, paying interest and taxes, and so on.
On the other hand, purchasing equipment or vehicles, or setting up
an IT infrastructure are done infrequently. These are called non-
recurring expenses.

Such significant investments are also known as capital
expenditures or CAPEX.

Example: A company bought a new fleet of vehicles for the Sales
Department this year. If accountants included the total amount
spent as an expense in the current period's income statement, it
would imply two things:

a) That the company consumed the full value of those vehicles and
at the end of the year their value is zero - which is not true. Ideally,
those assets will be used over several accounting periods.

b) Because such spending represents a large investment, it might
cause the company go into loss.

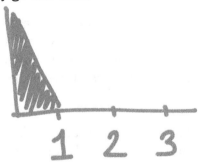

Depreciation helps the company calculate the remaining value of
the asset, treating as an expense only the portion of the asset that
was used during the current period.

The depreciation is only an estimate. Going back to the last example, even if all the salespeople used the same type of vehicle, their driving styles are likely so different that in three years the condition of each vehicle will also be different. However, in the financial statements their value will be the same.

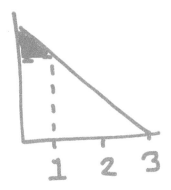

There are several methods to determine depreciation (see the illustrations below), including:
- Straight line
- Declining balance
- Depreciation per usage (per cycle, per item produced, per mileage, etc.)

Depreciation is known as a non-cash expense because the cash is usually spent when the equipment is initially purchased. After that, the equipment's value decreases each period (it depreciates), but the company does not pay any cash as the owner of this asset.

Income statement ratios

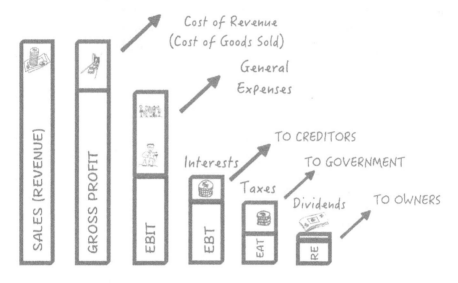

Ratios are a fundamental part of financial statement analysis. By examining an income statement, more than seven ratios can be calculated:

Gross profit, also known as sales profit or gross margin, is the difference between revenue and the direct cost of producing the merchandise. This ratio measures the fundamental profitability of an operation without taking into consideration other expenses such as administration, interest, sales costs, and taxes.

If the gross profit of a company is declining from year to year, this might indicate one or more of the following:
- Sales volume is decreasing
- The business is not charging enough for its products
- The cost of raw materials is increasing
- The production process is not efficient (for example there are losses because of aging equipment).

EBITDA (earnings before interest, taxes, depreciation, and amortization). As the name suggests, this ratio measures the performance of the company by including all expenses except interest, the cost of using assets (depreciation and amortization), and taxes.

EBIT (earnings before interest and taxes). This ratio is calculated by subtracting from sales all expenses except interest and taxes. It is similar to the EBITDA.

Interest. The amount that creditors (banks) charge a business for the privilege of using their money.

Taxes. The amount payable to the government.

EAT (earning after tax, also known as net income or net profit). The EAT is the difference between the value a company produces (sales) and the value it consumes (all expenses), and is used to measure the success of the company.

Dividends. A business might share the net profit or part of it with the investors by paying dividends.

RE (retained earnings). This measures what is left after dividends are paid. If a company does not pay dividends, the RE will equal the EAT.

EBIT(DA) vs. net profit

Net income is sales minus all expenses. EBITDA leaves out interest, taxes, and depreciation.

EBITDA is not a financial measurement accepted by the Generally Accepted Accounting Practices (GAAP) and has been criticized because it doesn't portray a realistic performance; interest, taxes, and depreciation are not directly related to the value process of a company.

Still, companies often focus their reporting on EBITDA, and for good reason.

Management has some control over sales; they can determine pricing and promotion campaigns, launch new products, open new markets, and so on.

A company's executives also have power over all types of expenses: cost of goods sold (COGS) and selling, general and administrative (SG&A). Decisions can be made to hire or fire people, to optimize the production process, or to switch to a more efficient provider.

However, management has little or no control over interest rates and taxes.

Management's Span of Control

This is one of the reasons why businesses seldom focus on reporting EBITDA, because this measurement minimizes the impact of factors outside of their scope of control and focuses on what can be controlled.

EBITDA has another advantage. It cancels the impact of country-specific variables. Taxes and interest rates vary in different economies, so dismissing their impact helps compare operations across borders more fairly.

Fixed and variable expenses

Expenses can also be classified as fixed or variable.

In a business, *variable cost* is proportional to the volume of product or service produced and usually includes raw materials, direct labor, distribution, and storage. The more output a company generates, the higher the variable cost will be. And if production stops, then the variable cost will be zero.

Example: If you are running a restaurant business, then your variable costs include everything related to preparing the food. The more customers you have in a given month, the more should be spent on raw materials such as ingredients.

This relation is not always strictly proportional. In an economy of scale, the cost variable should decrease as production rises.

In another uncommon scenario, the opposite could be true: imagine selling a product that is based on a limited supply of raw materials, so that with each product the cost would increase.

Fixed costs are not related to the production.
Going back to the restaurant example, it doesn't matter whether you have many or few customers; you would still pay rent, utilities, salaries to waiters and administrative staff, and advertising.

However, it is likely that fixed costs vary too. If your business is growing significantly, you might consider renting another facility or hiring more personnel. On the other hand, if the company is performing poorly, you might consider firing part of your staff or reducing your marketing budget.

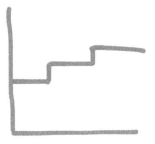

The distinction between fixed and variable costs is sometimes not so obvious and depends on the industry and financial policy for recognizing expenses.

For a retail business, electricity could be a fixed cost because you will pay the same bill whether your store is full of customers or empty. However, for a manufacturing company, electricity could represent a variable cost because it is a manufacturing cost and it would increase significantly as production increases.

Cost of Revenue

R&D

Selling General and
Administrative

Interest

Net Profit

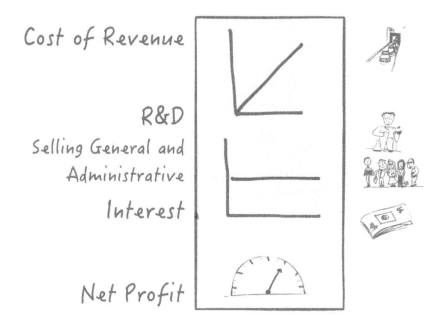

Break-even point

The total cost is the sum of variable and fixed costs.

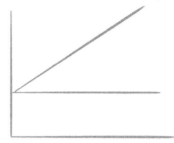

By filling in the chart below with your company's real numbers, you could estimate what percentage of expenses is fixed and what percentage is a variable cost, according to production volume.

In the same way that costs can be estimated, you can also predict the revenue you will earn by selling a particular volume. The sales line represents this.

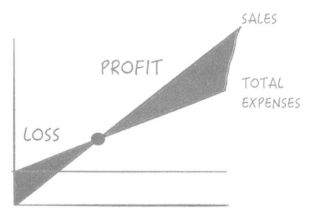

The difference between sales and total costs is the profit (blue area) or the loss (red zone).

The break-even point analysis is a visual way to represent information from the income statement, and can be used to:
- Improve pricing
- Calculate the point of profitability
- Try different scenarios

Not all businesses are equally profitable

Some businesses are more profitable than others. For each dollar, euro, peso, yen, or whatever currency they charge for a sale, those companies are left with a higher portion of profit.

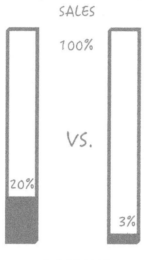

SALES

100%

VS.

20%

3%

NET PROFIT

The most profitable industries include healthcare, IT services, financial services, and telecommunications.

Company	Net Profit %
Apple	22% *(2015)*
Microsoft	25% *(2014)*
Pfizer	18% *(2014)*
The Coca-Cola Company	15% *(2014)*
Citigroup	10% *(2014)*
IBM	13% *(2014)*
Merck	26% *(2014)*

There are several common reasons for this higher profitability. Those companies:
- have a strong brand (The Coca-Cola Company)

- hold a stable position which makes it harder for them to be replaced by a competitor (Microsoft Office)
- invest heavily in research & development and offer a patented product without viable substitution (Pfizer)

Another reason for the success of this group of companies might be that they base their price on what the customer is willing to pay rather than on the real cost. Take a software company, for example. If you sell a product via download, once you reach your break-even point, each copy you sell doesn't translate equally in cost. In other words, your cost for each additional sale is close to zero. Still, you will likely charge a price higher than zero.

If you are not unique, you better be cheap

Another group of companies has a lower percentage of profits. These industries include food, utilities, manufacturing, airlines, and logistics.

Company	Net Profit %	
Exxon Mobil	8%	(2014)
Ford	2%	(2014)
ConAgra Foods	2%	(2014)
Wal-Mart	3%	(2015)
Delta Airlines	1.6%	(2014)
Costco	2%	(2015)

The reason for that might be that customers are more price-conscious, or the competition is more aggressive.

It does not necessary mean that the businesses from this second group are less successful than the first one. Pfizer generates a profit that is 18% of sales, while Wal-Mart's profit margin is only 3%. But because Wal-Mart's sales volume is much higher, in the end the 3% ($16,363,000) represents more than Pfizer's 18% ($9,135,000).

It is important for a business to know the average profitability of the industry in which it operates, so management will understand if the company is underperforming or overachieving.

Putting it all together: visual income statements from different industries

Following are four visual income statement examples from different industries.

Apple Inc. (NASDAQ:AAPL)

Apple's gross profit is 40%. This means that when you buy an Apple product, the average direct cost is 60%. Apple spends heavily on R&D and marketing, which represents almost the entire fixed cost of 18%.

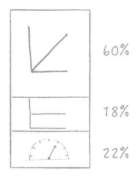

60%

18%

22%

Pfizer Inc. (NYSE:PFE)

The ratios for Pfizer are typical of the pharmaceutical industry. While the direct cost of the product is relatively low (18%), the company spends heavily on research and administrative expenses, which leads to a general expense of 64%.

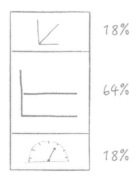

18%

64%

18%

Delta Airlines, Inc. (NYSE:DAL)

The airline industry has experienced very aggressive competition over the last few years. Prices have slightly increased, just to cover the effect of inflation. As you can see from the chart, when you buy an airline ticket the direct cost of your travel is (on average) 55%. Airlines also have high fixed costs. An aircraft costs a fortune, and airlines operate with very high leasing expenses.

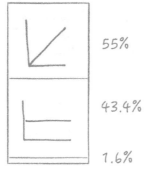

55%

43.4%

1.6%

Ford Motor Co. (NYSE:F)

The automotive industry is currently facing tough price competition. As you can see from the chart, when you buy a vehicle it costs Ford 84% of the sales price to manufacture and deliver your new car. With the remaining 16%, the company needs to pay marketing expenses, research and development, administrative expenses, interest, and so on, and still be left with a profit.

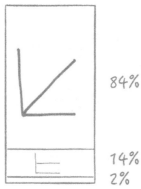

84%

14%
2%

Abstract:

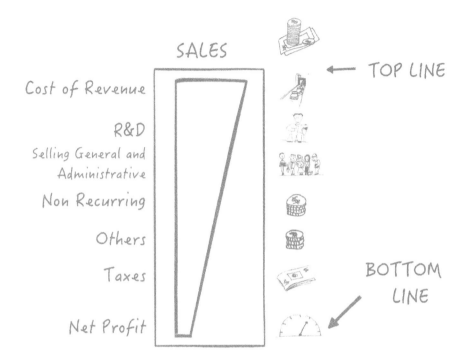

The right side of the one-page model represents how a business is doing:

- Starting with the sales volume at the top
- Listing the different expenses (COGS, SG&A, taxes, interest)
- Finishing with the net profit at the bottom

This page intentionally left blank.

Cash: the missing link

Cash is what connects the balance sheet and the income statement, and is what drives a business. Cash flows in from customers after a sale and it pays providers and salaries.

- Use of assets generates cash through revenue.
- Producing value also requires cash for expenses.
- Net profit (net income) flows into owner's equity via retained earnings.

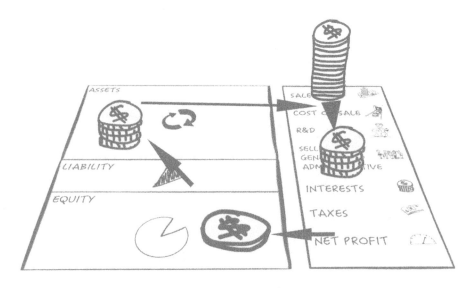

Cash vs. profit

Both profit and cash are important for a business's success. If a company is not profitable during a particular period, investors will definitely be unhappy. Nonetheless, if the business has enough cash, it will survive and eventually become successful. This is especially true for startup companies. For instance, Amazon (NASDAQ:AMZN) ran at a loss for eight years before becoming profitable.

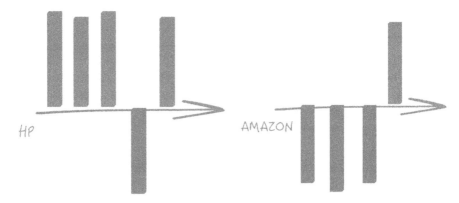

A different case is when an already profitable company suddenly experiences a loss. Hewlett Packard (NYSE:HPE) reported a stable annual profit until 2012, when the company lost $8.8 billion after it acquired the UK company Autonomy and discovered that Autonomy overstated profit by 80%. In cases like this, investors are unhappy and somebody usually loses their job. However, a company with enough cash survives, as HP did.

However, survival is not guaranteed for the business that runs out of cash. When this happens, the corporation cannot pay its expenses, because only liquid assets are accepted. Salaries are put on hold. Providers don't get their money and stop delivering. Operations are interrupted. Management is discharged. The company files for bankruptcy.

There are several options for injecting cash into a business. However, they require precious time and may or may not work. The management could:

- Sell assets, though this may damage the company's future capacity to produce value.
- Borrow more money, though it's unlikely that banks will be open to helping a business with cash trouble.
- Charge customers more quickly. This will work only if there are sufficient accounts receivable and if customers are willing to co-operate quickly.

Infrequently, an organization with liquidity difficulties can recover. Healing may involve restructuring, and the resulting new company is usually smaller. In most cases, a business with cash problems will never be operational again, and owners may consider splitting units and selling the profitable ones.

Smart investors also focus their attention on cash rather than profit alone for several reasons:

- Profitability can be fixed over time if the business has firm roots, but cash problems are usually a sign that the end is coming.
- Cash is harder to manipulate. While the income statement uses many estimates and can be subject to deliberate manipulation, cash is easily measured because it is backed by what's in bank accounts.

Not having enough cash is bad for a business. Keeping too much cash is also problematic, for the following reasons:

- Money is not invested in operation and is not providing the return a company expects, as banks are not paying high interest rates right now. Most businesses produce a higher return on capital employed than they would by keeping funds in savings account.

- Abundant cash makes it is easier to spend on unnecessary extravagances.
- Investors expect their fair share.

The good news is that there's a dedicated financial statement to help understand cash and prevent situations like those mentioned above.

Cashflow statement and income statement

The cash flow statement shows us something that the income statement does not: when an action actually affects cash.

We mentioned before that a sale is recognized when a good or service is delivered. However, it may be some time before the sale is actually charged. In some cases, payment may be received in a different accounting period.

The same thing applies to costs. A company may pre-pay certain expenses or pay providers in a later accounting period.

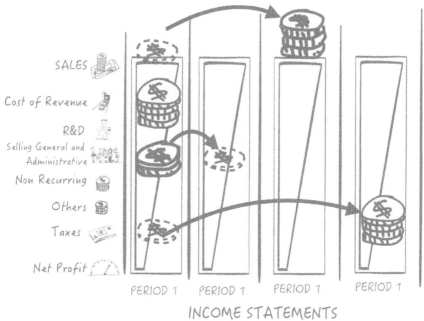

INCOME STATEMENTS

Such shifts are part of a normal business operation. However, in these cases the income statement will reflect a change (you recognized a sale), but cash will be not affected, as payment wasn't received. When you receive the payment later, the cash statement will change (you received money, a cash inflow), but the income statement won't change (because the sale was already recognized during a previous period).

This example could even be used to "cook" the books by switching expenses or revenue from one period to another. We'll cover this topic in a succeeding chapter.

In a nutshell, the cash flow statement helps us discover when (and if) an operation reported in the income statement affects cash: when sales were actually charged and when expenses were actually paid.

Introducing the cash flow statement

The cash flow statement (also known as statement of cash flow) is the third important and mandatory financial report.

A company's financial statements are interrelated. The balance sheet tells us what assets the company has. The income statement reveals how a business is using said assets to produce value. The cash flow statement is linked to both, as well as the cash generated and used during that period.

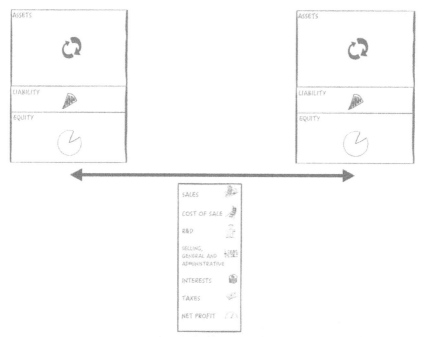

Information about money movement can be obtained from two balance sheets (at the beginning and end of an accounting period) plus the income statement.

However, the calculations involved are impractical and can be hard to understand, which is why public companies must include cash flow statement as a separate document in their annual report.

The cash flow statement has three main parts:
- Operating activities show the cash the company generated or used while producing a product or a service.
- Investing activities reflect the acquisition of long-term assets such as machinery or properties.
- Financial activities include loans the company takes out, changes in debt, and dividends or interest paid.

The cash flow statement provides information about:
- Cash position. The amount of money a company has at the end of the period in all its bank accounts and all currencies.
- Cash flow. The difference between the amount of cash at the beginning vs. the end of the accounting period.

Who uses the cash flow statement most? Information about how a corporation manages its cash is treasured by:
- The accounting department. It must ensure that the company will have enough cash to pay its financial obligations.
- Stakeholders. As mentioned earlier, investors often dig deeper into how a company manages money rather than looking only at its current profitability.
- Creditors. Banks analyze a client's cash flow statement before authorizing new credit.
- Providers and employees. Both groups can verify the company's ability to pay.

Inflows and outflows

What is the impact of decisions on cash?

When we discuss cash, we're talking about cash inflows and outflows.

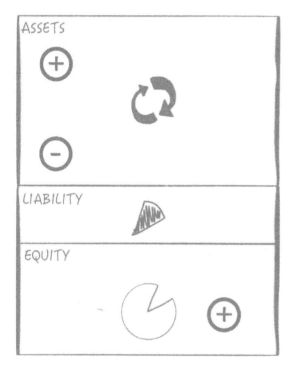

- Inflows are when you receive cash, perhaps by charging customers or selling an asset.
- Outflows are when cash leaves your company, for instance when you pay providers or purchase equipment.

The cash flow statement is not about the absolute values of what a company has (we have the balance sheet for that), but about variations.

Whether a variation is an inflow or outflow depends on how the operation affects cash: positively (receiving cash) or negatively (spending cash). Here are some examples:

- Selling equipment is an inflow because you will earn cash.
- Raising inventory levels is an outflow because the more inventory a company has, the less free cash it will have available.
- Repaying debt is an outflow because liabilities are paid with liquid assets.
- Buying equipment is an outflow if it is purchased using cash.
- Depreciation is a non-cash expense. Cash is usually paid at the beginning, when the equipment is purchased.

Examples of cash inflows and outflows by category

INFLOW

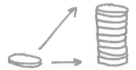

Operating activities:
- Selling goods or services to customers
- Selling marketable securities

Investing activities:
- Collecting loans
- Selling property or equipment
- Selling short-term or long-term investments

Financing activities:
- Selling stock
- Issuing of debt

OUTFLOW

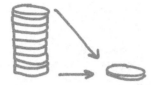

Operating activities:
- Paying taxes
- Paying interests
- Paying expenses (such as salaries, R&D, marketing)
- Purchasing inventory

Investing activities:
- Making loans
- Purchasing property, plants, or equipment

Financing activities
- Repaying debt
- Paying dividends
- Acquiring common stock

Application: examining a cash flow statement

Apple Inc. (NASDAQ:AAPL)

	2015	
Net Income	**53,394,000**	
Operating Activities		
Depreciation	11,257,000	+
Adjustments To Net Income	4,968,000	+
Changes In Accounts Receivables	(3,124,000)	-
Changes In Liabilities	15,188,000	+
Changes In Inventories	(238,000)	-
Changes In Other Operating Activities	(179,000)	-
Total Cash Flow From Operating Activities	**81,266,000**	+
Investing Activities		
Capital Expenditures	(11,247,000)	-
Investments	(44,417,000)	-
Other Cash flows from Investing Activities	(610,000)	-
Total Cash Flows From Investing Activities	**(56,274,000)**	-
Financing Activities		
Dividends Paid	(11,561,000)	-
Sale Purchase of Stock	(34,710,000)	-
Net Borrowings	29,305,000	+
Other Cash Flows from Financing Activities	(1,499,000)	-
Total Cash Flows From Financing Activities	**(17,716,000)**	-
Change In Cash and Cash Equivalents	**7,276,000**	+

The cash conversion cycle

Cash and time

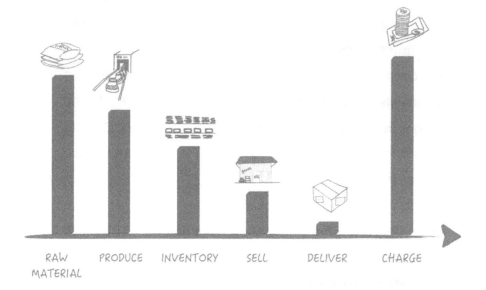

RAW MATERIAL · PRODUCE · INVENTORY · SELL · DELIVER · CHARGE

The cash convention cycle (CCC) measures the time in days that a company needs to wait to recover the cash invested in operations.

For a manufacturing company, for example, the way to calculate CCC is as follows:

Time in inventory (how many days production takes, from the time a provider delivers raw materials until the finished product is sold and delivered)

+

How many days it takes for the company to collect payment (what are the credit terms)

–

How many days it takes for the business to pay providers

The cash conversion cycle time varies from industry to industry. It's common for a manufacturing company to have CCC with a duration of more than 30 days. For example, a car manufacturer needs more than six months to convert raw materials to a car, sell it, deliver it, and charge it. A retailer, on the other hand, will sometimes complete its cycle in fewer than seven days, or more than 25 times faster.

Analyzing the cash conversion cycle for your business helps you study and manage the cash flow and estimate cash needs. Having a CCC of 300 days, for example, is not necessarily a bad thing if it's the norm for your industry. However, you should plan and search for financing early to avoid being left without cash before delivering and charging for the product.

For more on how to accurately calculate CCC, please go to page 124.

Cash flow and timing

The value of money decreases with time. $5 can buy more goods today than in ten years. Perhaps it can buy a large coffee now, but in several years the same amount of money will have lost value and you will barely be able to buy a small coffee.

$5

When considering cash flow over several years, you must account for the time factor, or your estimate will not be credible.

Imagine you need to invest $500,000 over three years and you have two options.

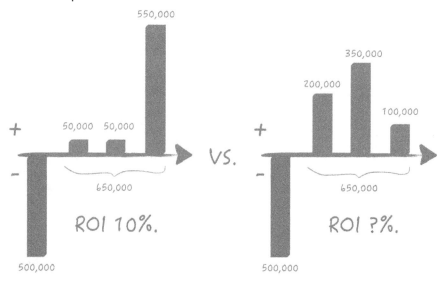

The first option is to put money in long-term investment plan with 10% annual return (see chart). In this scenario, during the first two years you receive the interest rate ($50,000), and the final third year you receive the initial investment plus the corresponding interest ($550,000). The total amount you get in return is $650,000.

You're presented with another investment opportunity, this time to develop a new product. The initial capital is the same ($500,000), and in the end, you receive the same amount as in the previous example ($650,000). However, in the second example the cash flow timing is different ($200,000 in Year 1, $350,000 in Year 2, and $100,000 in Year 3).

Both opportunities appear similar because what you invest and what you receive in three years is the same. Which one is better, or is there even a difference?

The main distinction is when the cash is received. In the first case, most of the cash is received later, which means that it has already lost some of its purchasing power. In the second example, however, more cash is collected sooner.

To calculate the exact return in the second case, each year's inflow must be multiplied by its discount factor. The discount rate is the multiplier by which future cash can be calculated to obtain its present value.

After doing the math, you discover that the real return in the second example is 15.5%. (Please refer to the bibliography section if you want to know more about calculating net present value.)

Although the two examples seem similar, the difference in return of more than 5% is a significant point for the second investment. If you're dealing with an important multimillion dollar project and you don't include an estimate of the time value of money, your credibility might be at risk.

Abstract:

The cash flow statement is the third mandatory financial report. It is not about what a company has (the balance sheet provides that information), nor whether the business is doing well or poorly (the income statement presents that data).

The cash flow statement details how much cash is generated and paid during an accounting period, and how much money the business is left with at the end.

The cash flow statement is mainly used by accounting personnel to establish whether the company can meet its obligations now and in the future. Investors are also very interested in cash because, as mentioned before, a lack of cash can derail a business.

What's behind the numbers

How to read financial statements

An analogy can be made between the financial reports of a company and the flight instruments in the cockpit of an airplane. Both provide essential information.

In the case of a plane, there are six main indicators in every type of aircraft: airspeed, attitude, altimeter, vertical speed, heading, and turn. Those represent the most useful information a pilot needs to have at all times. In the same way, a decision maker in a company needs the vital information from the income statement, the balance sheet, and the cash flow statement.

Still, you might wonder why the modern aircraft has more than 350 buttons, gauges, lights, and switches if flying an airplane requires only six instruments. These provide additional information, which is sometimes more important than that provided by the main six indicators.
If a pilot ignores a landing gear failure indicator, he and the passengers are headed for trouble during the landing. On the other hand, recognizing the problem in time and preparing the crew significantly increases the chances of a successful emergency landing.

Similar to the 350-plus lights in a commercial aircraft, financial ratios offer a way to obtain vital information about a company's health.

Horizontal and vertical analysis

Vertical analysis is demonstrated on page 61 when comparing different expenses as a percentage of sales.

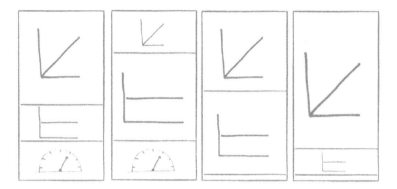

Horizontal analysis is when you compare results not as a percentage of a total, but as a change between periods.

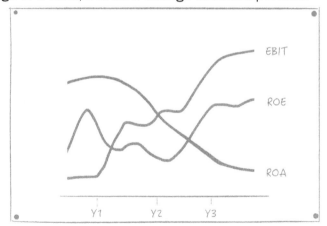

Some of the items that might provide valuable information when compared are:

 • Changes in revenue and what causes them.
 • Changes in expenses. Are providers charging more? How is inflation affecting your business?
 • Changes in assets and the balance of those assets. Do you have more inventory and less cash?
 • Changes in debt. Is the company's debt increasing over time, and why?

Getting more from the balance sheet

The income statement can help us define:
- How profitable is the business?
- How efficient is the production process?
- How efficient are providers?
- What percentage is the company paying for salaries?
- What value does each employee create in the company?
- What is the return on investment in marketing and sales?

The balance sheet, however, can help us better understand the financial position of the company.

For example, you could use vertical analysis to calculate the percentage of cash related to the total assets.

Even more complex financial ratios can be calculated using only the balance sheet, to help you obtain additional valuable information.

The illustration of the balance sheet below includes the assets (current and fixed) on one side and the liabilities (current and non-current) plus equity on the other side.

For the sake of the demonstration, let's use the numbers from the 2014 Starbucks (NASDAQ:SBUX) balance sheet, available in their 2014 annual report.

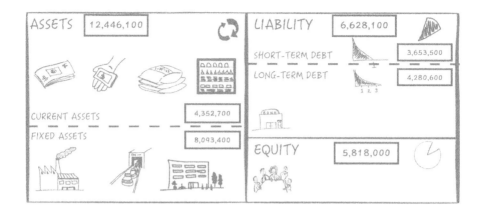

For the investors and management of Starbucks, this balance sheet provides knowledge about:

- What is the asset strength?
- How is the company funded? What part belongs to the owners and what part to creditors?
- How much money does the corporation have right now?
- Is the business able to pay its debts?
- Is the business carrying too much debt?
- Does the company have the resources to sustain growth?
- Is the company taking advantage of the assets it has?
- What is the capital employed?
- Will the business have enough cash to pay debt?
- How much of the inventory is rotated per year?
- How many days does it take to charge, on average?

Now let's see what those specific numbers can tell us.

Can you pay your short-term obligations?

Liquidity ratios help you determine if a company will be able to pay its short term (current) obligations when they are due.

Current ratio

To calculate this ratio, divide all the current assets by the current liabilities. In general terms, it answers the question "How many times can we pay what we owe right now using all our current assets (inventory, cash, accounts receivable), and excluding all fixed assets such as property, plant and equipment?"

In this example, for Starbucks, the current ratio is 1.37, meaning that for each dollar of debt, Starbucks has $1.37 in assets to repay it. A ratio higher than one shows a stronger financial position. If the current ratio is less than one, it means that the company might not have sufficient resources to pay its debt without having to charge customers or sell assets.

However, a current ratio of less than one does not necessarily indicate a problem. Sometimes numbers as low as 0.5 are standard for industries that move cash slowly or have too much inventory.

A high current ratio might show that the business is not using its current assets efficiently.

Quick ratio

This ratio excludes the inventory and is calculated by dividing cash plus accounts receivables by current liabilities, thus concentrating on the most liquid assets such as cash and receivables.

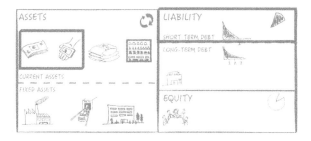

The quick ratio is also known as the "acid test" ratio because it excludes inventory.

Inventory is a "current asset," but it is not as liquid as management sometimes wishes it were. For example, an inventory might have an expiration date (typical for medicine and food) and if for some reason it's not sold on time, the company will have to write it off.

In 2013, Sanofi's "Brazil generic issue" led to selling a lot of inventory at a discount until it started to expire, at which point the company recorded a write-off of 79 million euros.

Other inventory such as technology is a subject to rapid change in customer preferences and competitor's moves.
Hewlett-Packard recorded a record $3.3 billion write-off in 2011 for its TouchPad after unsuccessfully competing on the tablet market. Amazon took a $170 million write-off because of unsold Fire Phones.

For Starbucks, the quick ratio number is 0.09

But how should we interpret it? Again, similar logic applies. A number less than one may indicate that the company is not able to repay its current liabilities using only cash and accounts receivable.

The higher the ratio, the better the company's liquidity. However, a too-large number may indicate an inefficient use of assets.

Cash ratio

The most conservative liquidity ratio is the cash ratio. It takes into consideration only the cash and excludes inventory and accounts receivable.

Similar to excessive inventory, being stuck with too many receivables represents a risk because there is no guarantee that the company will be able to convert inventory and accounts receivable to cash in time to repay its debt.

If a corporation is too slow in charging (usually a matter of months, not days), money loses its purchasing power. If the economy goes bad, more customers may default on their credit.

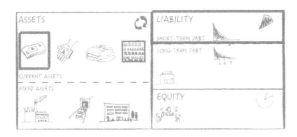

For Starbucks the cash ratio is 0.56, meaning that by the time the financial report was published, the company could not pay its current debt with only the cash available.

However, this is typical for a business. Few industries have enough cash to cover their debt without having to count on selling inventory or converting receivables to cash.

A healthy cash ratio is considered to be between 0.5 and 1.

Liquidity ratios are helpful way to measure if a company is at risk of not being able to pay its debt. However, some critics point out that those ratios are past-oriented and cannot predict future cash problems.

Also, such ratios can be misleading because of creative accounting practices (a topic we will cover later on), especially because accounts receivable might be inflated or inventory could be wrongly estimated.

How indebted is your company?

Debt-to-equity

Every company is funded by two main sources, owner's equity and debt. The debt-to-equity ratio measures the balance between those two and tells you how much debt you use to run the business.

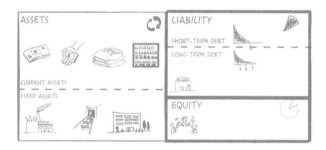

For Starbucks, the debt-to-equity ratio is 1.03 which means that for a dollar of equity Starbucks has approximately a dollar of debt. For most companies a normal range is between 0.8 and 1.1

Technology Healthcare Retail Consumer Services Utilities Financial

How much debt is good?

Debt brings risk. Some companies or industries have little debt. Facebook (NASDAQ: FB) for example has a debt-to-equity ratio of 0.11.

On the other hand, some industries require a lot of capital and use more debt to finance their activities.

While discussing the cash conversion cycle earlier, we mentioned that some businesses need a lot of time to turn an investment into a successful product. This is true for construction, machinery, and utilities, to name a few.

Boeing's (NYSE: BA) debt-to-equity ratio is 10.44, which means that to finance its operations, it has $10.40 of debt for each dollar of owner's equity.

The banking and financial services also relies on a lot of debt, because they essentially borrow money to lend money.

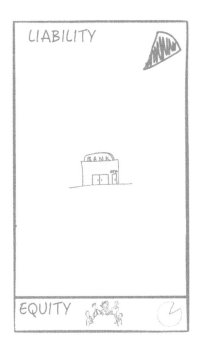

Is debt a bad thing?

Not necessarily. Debt costs money because a business must pay interest for it, as opposed to financing operations with equity.

However, using one's own capital is not usually enough to grow quickly, especially in low margin industries. If a company wants to expand in a more aggressive way, it needs to finance itself through liability.

Using debt to finance assets is called leverage. By using leverage, a company increases the available capital without growing its equity.

In the example above, a company has $1 million in assets and generates $50,000 in profit. Management then decides to borrow $1 million more, and now they have twice the assets ($2 million) and will eventually produce two times the profit. The owners double the profit without investing more of their money; ergo, leverage.

Can you pay your interest?

Interest coverage ratio

Debt can multiply the chances of success and growth, but it also costs money in interest payments.

Another useful ratio measures how easily a company can pay the interest generated from its liability.

For Starbucks this number is 50, which means the company can pay 50 times its interest expense with the result (EBIT) it generated during this financial period.

If this number gets closer to 1, it means the company can hardly pay its interest expense. 2.5 is considered a warning sign.

The interest coverage ratio measures the short-term financial health of the company.

Working capital vs. capital employed

Working capital

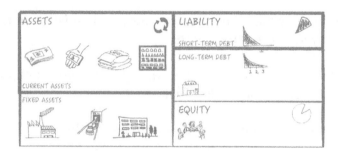

The working capital, also known as the current capital, is money an organization can use for day-to-day operations.

Working capital = current assets – current liabilities

For Starbucks, this is 1,130,000,000 or 1.13 billion. Working capital is not easy to compare between companies or industries because different businesses have different cash needs. However, the working capital is related to the current ratio discussed on page 104, which can be more practically compared.

Capital employed

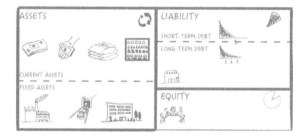

The capital employed is calculated by adding the fixed assets to the working capital. It's the money owners and shareholders have invested in the business. For Starbucks, the number is 5,288,700.

Profitability and management effectiveness

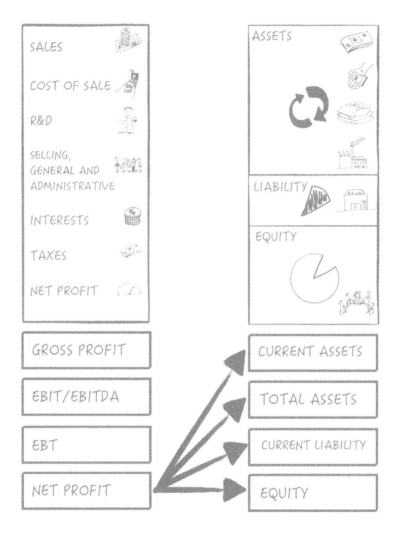

Until now we have explored different ways to measure profitability such as EBIT, EBITDA, and EAT using the income statement.

Nevertheless, this information didn't disclose how the company is using its assets to produce this value or if the company is taking maximum advantage of its assets.

The balance sheet provides relevant information about the company's health, liquidity, asset strength, and debt.

Combining information from the income statement and the balance sheet gives us an additional, broader perspective about management effectiveness.

ROA: is the company taking the best advantage of assets?

ROA is calculated by dividing the net profit by total assets. For Starbucks, ROA is 17.45%, which means that each $100 of the company's assets generates $17.45 in net profit annually.

Each industry has a different usage of assets. For example, a service company can generate many more sales with fewer assets than a manufacturing company. This is why the ROA should be compared within the industry context.

The more asset-intensive the company is, the lower the ROA.

Examples of ROA values: Retail – 15%, Restaurants – 12%, Biotechnology and drugs – 10%, Professional services – 9%, Software and programming – 7.5%, Construction – 7%, Airlines – 5%, Hotels and leisure – 5%, Utilities – 2 to 3%, Rental and leasing – 2%, Auto and truck manufacturers – 2%, Banks – 1% and less, Iron and Steel – 0.4%).

Having a higher ROA may be a sign that management is using assets efficiently. Though as in many financial ratios, beware of anything that sounds "too good to be true." If a company's ROA is higher than the industry norm, it may be a warning that the company is not renewing its assets (i.e., investing in equipment) and may soon need to make that investment to stay competitive.

ROE: how efficiently is the company using owner's equity?

The return on equity (ROE) measures what amount of profit is returned as a percentage of the owner's equity. In other words, this ratio tells us what the investors earned for their venture.

ROE = Net Profit / Equity

For Starbucks, this ratio is 49%.

However, the ROE has one weakness. If a business uses a lot of debt to finance its assets, then the ROE will be very high because the denominator (equity) will be low (more debt means less equity).

So in such cases ROE might be misleading.

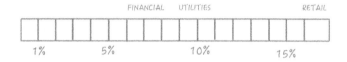

Examples of ROE values: Retail – 17%, Utilities – 9%, Financial – 8%

ROCE: are you getting the best return on your investment

As mentioned above, the ROE's weakness is that it only takes into consideration the equity of a company, not accounting for the proportion of debt.

The return of capital employed (ROCE) fixes this problem because it takes into consideration the fixed assets (i.e., the investment that is employed to produce value).

As shown previously, capital employed is calculated by adding working capital to the fixed assets.

ROCE, therefore, is calculated by dividing EBIT by the capital employed.

Efficiency ratios: how do you manage your business?

The following ratios measure how the company manages its processes such as production, delivery, collection of accounts receivable, and human resources.

Days sales in inventory (DSI)
How long does it take to sell your inventory?

DSI is also known as days in inventory (DII) or days inventory outstanding (DIO).

DSI = (Average Inventory) / (Cost of Goods Sold/365)

This ratio measures how long in days it takes for a company to convert its inventory into a sale.

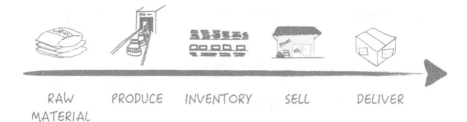

RAW MATERIAL   PRODUCE   INVENTORY   SELL   DELIVER

Keeping inventory in stock is expensive because a company needs to store and maintain it. There is always a risk that the inventory might not be sold (some examples were mentioned previously), so the more quickly the company moves its inventory, the better.

For Starbucks, the DSI is 52 days.

Inventory turnover

This ratio measures how many times per year a company sells its inventory.

The formula for inventory turnover is 360 / DSI.

For Starbucks, this is 6.92.

While again it depends on the industry, in most cases the inventory turnover ratio is between 6 and 12.

Examples: Cloud services – 261, Services – 30, Restaurants – 25, Technology – 10, Retail – 8, Food processing – 8, Utilities – 6, Mining – 5, Healthcare – 3, Aerospace and defense – 3, Construction – 1.64.

Low inventory turnover might be a sign of obsolete inventory, poor sales, weak inventory management, or an overstock of raw materials.

Some industries have low inventory turnover because of the type of business or limitations outside of management's control. For example, within the agriculture, mining, and construction industries, it takes time to grow a crop, extract a resource, or construct a building. This period is difficult or impossible to accelerate, so naturally inventory turnover will be lower.

Higher turnover is usually an indicator of good sales performance. However, a higher turnover might be a sign of trouble. It can mean that you have reduced cash flow and cannot afford to keep enough inventory. This may jeopardize future sales, as the company may not have enough stock to satisfy demand.

Some industries have a high turnover rate by nature because producing a product takes a short time or because the business has a low inventory level compared to the sales they generate (such as selling a copy of software or providing a web service).

DSO: how quickly is the company charging its customers?

Days sales outstanding (DSO) measures how many days on average a company takes to collect accounts receivable for sales that were delivered.

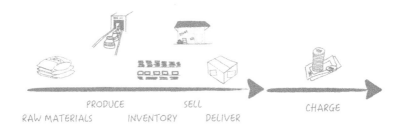

DSO = (Average Accounts Receivable) / (Sales/360)

SALES	ASSETS
COST OF SALE	
R&D	
SELLING, GENERAL AND ADMINISTRATIVE	LIABILITY
INTERESTS	EQUITY
TAXES	
NET PROFIT	

For Starbucks, DSO is 12.58 days.

The more quickly a business collects accounts receivable, the more cash the company will have available. Slow collection may indicate that the company is having trouble with receivables. Again, as with all ratios, this depends on the industry.
Businesses with principally cash transactions are faster in collecting. Some examples:
- Departmental and discount retail - 3.7 days
- Grocery stores - 5 days
- Technology - 8.7 days
- Restaurants - 12 days
- Airlines - 16 days
- Hotels - 24 days
- Utilities - 28 days
- Services - 32 days.

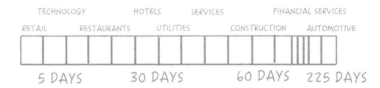

Other businesses are much slower in collecting. Examples include:

- Auto manufacturing - 225 days
- Financial services - 124 days
- Construction - 86 days
- Biotechnology and drugs - 60 days
- Professional services - 60 days.

DPO: how quickly do you pay providers?

Days Payable Outstanding (DPO) = Accounts payable at the end / (Cost of Goods Sold/Days)

For Starbucks, DPO is 28 days.

Most industries pay providers anywhere between 30 and 60 days. Yet it is not uncommon to see terms of more than 220 days. Finding the right balance of time to pay vendors helps a company maintain a healthy cash flow.

Paying too quickly could harm the liquidity of an organization. Paying too slowly could harm the providers' trust and jeopardize future deliveries. Sometimes corporations take advantage of a dominant position and pay providers slowly because the providers don't have other options for selling their product.

Long DPO could also indicate that a company is having liquidity problems and is unable to pay its debts, including to providers.

DPO is an average metric and might not give complete information. A company could be paying some providers on time (especially those delivering vital raw materials), while delaying payment for other products or services.

Cash conversion cycle (CCC)

The cash conversion cycle was previously covered (see page 95).

While it is actually a liquidity ratio and is used for cash-flow analysis, CCC is calculated by using the efficiency ratios (DIO, DSO, and DPO).

CCC = DIO + DSO – DPO

For Starbucks, CCC is 37 days.

It is not uncommon for a company to have a negative CCC, especially in the retail industry. This indicates that the company pays suppliers after it receives payment from a customer.

For example, Apple Inc. has a CCC of minus 57 days because they hold inventory for 6 days (DIO) (!), charge in 34 days (DSO), and pay providers in 98 days (DPO).

A higher CCC means better liquidity and less need to borrow money.

All the aforementioned ratios that involve inventory (DIO, DSO, DPO) and the CCC are most relevant for companies that actually manage inventory and will be less relevant (or irrelevant) to businesses that sell services.

How efficiently is the company engaging employees?

Even though employees are not an asset in the common meaning of the word, without question the way a company engages and uses people's knowledge and skills is one of the most critical success factors.

There is a ratio that measures how efficiently an employer uses its employees.

The revenue per employee is calculated by dividing the total sales by the number of staff. The more labor intensive the company is, the lower this ratio will be.

The range can be from $25,000 (restaurants) to more than $15 million per employee in some companies involved in trade, precious metals, and oil (examples include Transammonia, A-Mark Financial, J.D. Heiskell and Company, and Mansfield Oil).

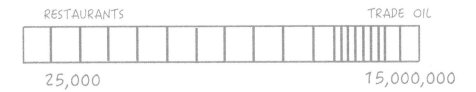

The revenue per employee can help you make better decisions about whether the company has enough workers.

What is the value of a company?

Have you ever considered buying a business? Or selling one? How do you define how much it's worth?

Book value

Imagine the following simplified balance sheet of a company
- Assets: 100
- Equity: 10
- Liability: 90

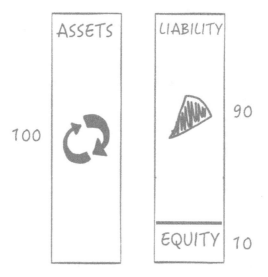

What is the value of the company?

You might guess that the value is 100 because this is what a company has. However, 90 out of those 100 are debt (claimed by banks).

So in this case, the theoretical (book) value of the company is 10.

But what is the "real" market price of a business?

Are people really an asset?

Make a list of all the resources that you company possesses and uses to produce value, for example:

- Property
- Patents
- Know-how
- Leadership
- People
- Culture
- Machinery
- Cash
- Accounts receivable
- Experience
- Reputation
- Brand

Now, cross off the list all the assets that a competitor can easily copy or buy.

You are probably left with such assets as:

culture, brand, reputation, leadership, and people

Most likely the items you kept are intangible and difficult to quantify. Such assets cannot be sold separately or don't have much value divided from the business.

Let's consider people. "Human capital is a company's most valuable asset" has turned into a common cliché. But it isn't true. Human resources do not meet the definition of an asset; the company does not materially own people and cannot sell them. Of course, employees have a central role in company's success, and they can have an impact on financial statements.

Yet even in sport clubs, players are not recognized as an asset, but rather accounted for by the amount the club paid to acquire the rights to use them. Athletes are not recognized as an asset in accounting.

A similar logic applies to brand, reputation, know-how (except for registered patents), and trust. These are things you will not find on a balance sheet.

And of course, they play a huge role in a company's success.

So if you decide to sell a business, you can charge a premium for these intangible factors, assuming that you offer a product or service with steady and growing demand.

MARKET VALUE

BOOK VALUE

How do you estimate the market value?

Public companies

For a public company, the way to estimate market capitalization is to multiply shares outstanding by the known value of those shares.

If the company in question is not public, you can compare it to a public company with a similar industry and sales.

Income valuation (discounted cash flows)

Another way to value the company is by calculating the future cash flow it will generate.

Following are some formulas for valuing a company based on its annual sales:

- Restaurant: 0.3 to 0.4 times annual sales plus inventory
- Supermarket: 0.15 times annual sales plus inventory
- Consulting business: 1 to 1.25 times annual sales
- Wellness and spa: 0.6 to 0.7 times annual sales

To arrive at a more definite number, you would need additional information such as the profitability of the company, annual sales growth, and profit growth.

Depending on the appraisal method used, two buyers might arrive at different values for the same company.

This shows that a considerable part of a company's value is based on the perceptions of the buyers about the risk and importance of the acquisition.

One of many notable examples: in 2014, Facebook paid $22 billion for WhatsApp, a company with five years' history that at that time generated $10.2 million in sales (note – sales, not profit!). Of course, Facebook must have had solid reasons to justify paying this price.

Company valuation is a complex topic; it requires detailed analysis and a dedicated team of experts. Even then, some acquisitions go wrong and cost millions or even billions in losses.

HP bought Palm for $1.2 billion. Cisco paid more than $500 million for Pure Digital, just to shut it down several years later. The AOL-Time Warner deal evaporated billions and according to many was the worst merger in business history.

The main hazards in company valuation include:
- Overestimating the growth potential
- Wrongly estimating risk
- Overbidding and overpaying, especially if the acquired assets are mostly intangible

How aligned is the organization?

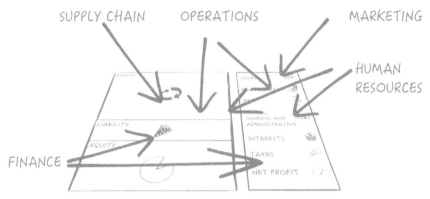

Though it's not always evident, all the departments within a company have the power to influence financial results.

Ask yourself whether your work can:
- Contribute to growing sales
- Help save expenses
- Increase profitability
- Use assets efficiently
- Help improve company's cash flow
- Charge customers more quickly
- Provide innovative ideas
- Reduce delivery times
- Improve customer service

(The more times you said yes, the more valuable are you to the company.)

The list could go on and on; those are just some examples of actions that can influence the company's financial statements.

In addition to the financial ratios for liquidity, efficiency, and profitability previously covered, each department develops and uses different metrics. Those key performance indicators (KPI) are used to measure the department's execution of and alignment with global company objectives. Here are some examples:

Sales and marketing:
- Market share
- Net promoter score
- Customer turnover
- Sales per salesperson
- Customer satisfaction/loyalty rate
- Brand equity

Operations:
- Rework percentage
- Manufacturing critical path time
- Productivity index
- Machine downtime percentage
- Maintenance expenses
- On time delivery ratio
- Waste levels

Logistics:
- Schedule accuracy
- On time delivery percentage
- Average time to deliver
- Inventory accuracy

Human Resources:
- Employee turnover
- Average time to fill a position
- Cost per hire
- Employee satisfaction/engagement index
- Absenteeism
- Salary competitiveness factor
- Training return on investment

Corporate social responsibility:
- Carbon and water footprint
- Energy consumption
- Product recycling rate
- Waste recycling rate

Is your company growing well?

The next two ratios are more strategic and less practical, yet interesting enough to mention.

We explained previously that a company with no cash is headed for trouble, whereas too much cash can be a sign of inefficiently used resources.

But what about growth? Not growing is bad, but can too much growth be dangerous too?

To grow more quickly requires cash, especially in a capital-intensive business. The money for expansion can come either from an external loan or from the owners.

There is a ratio for growth, too. The growth equilibrium is an interesting yet rather theoretical strategic quotient. It measures whether a company can sustain positive growth with its operating cash flow.

It was first suggested in 1977 paper titled "How Much Growth Can a Firm Afford?"

If you want to know more about this ratio, please consult the bibliography.

Is your company headed for bankruptcy?

Another impressive ratio is Altman Z-Score. Discovered in 1968 by Edward Altman, this quotient measures the probability of a company going into bankruptcy within two years.

Over the last few decades, the formula has proven to be highly accurate. It was originally developed for public manufacturing companies, with other versions for private and non-manufacturing organizations becoming available later.

The original Z-Score formula was as follows:

$$Z = 1.2X_1 + 1.4X_2 + 3.3X_3 + 0.6X_4 + 0.99X_5.$$

Where:
- $X1$ = Working Capital / Total Assets
- $X2$ = Retained Earnings / Total Assets
- $X3$ = Earnings Before Interest and Taxes / Total Assets.
- $X4$ = Market Value of Equity / Book Value of Total Liabilities.
- $X5$ = Sales / Total Assets.

If $Z > 2.99$, the company is in the Safe Zone.
A Z-Score between 1.81 and 2.99 is in the Gray Zone.
If $Z < 1.81$, the business is in the Distress Zone and will most likely go bankrupt within two years.

COMPANY 1   COMPANY 2

Another interesting thing about the Z-Score is that by combining several ratios and multiplying them with different weights, it manages to reduce a company to a single number that helps compare companies across industries.

Making better decisions

Making better decisions

Have you ever thought how many decisions you make in a single day? Research says you can make over 200 daily decisions about food alone.

The more you advance within an organization, the more impact your decisions will have. Ultimately all your choices will translate into financial results: sales, costs, profitability, and cash flow.

It's not only top management who influence results.
- A customer service representative with a poor judgment can lose a very profitable customer.
- Wrong invoices generated by the accounting department must be re-issued, which can cause a delay in charging customers and negatively affect cash flow.
- An HR manager who fails to recruit the right talent the first time contributes to increased costs.

Speaking of results, according to the income statement (which measures productivity) the ultimate objectives are to:
- Sell more (top line)
- Decrease costs: cost of goods sold, general expenses, taxes, and interest (bottom line)

Both objectives will result in increased profit.

The balance sheet also gives priorities for improvement. Some of the goals here are to:
- Improve usage of resources
- Improve cash flow
- Improve liquidity

Sell more

Selling more can be interpreted in different ways:
- Increase the price but sell the same number of products or services
- Grow the number sold without changing the price
- Or both.

Several signs can indicate that your company has a revenue problem. For example, your sales are growing slower than the competition's. You are forced to lower prices. The company's market share is shrinking. The business depends on very few key customers. Clients are also experiencing financial problems.

Growing revenue is not an easy task, especially in a mature and competitive market. It usually requires a significant investment, and results take time.

Costs could include increasing sales through the internet, finding new distribution channels, and improving promotional materials.

Reduce costs

If your gross margin is steadily declining, it's a warning sign that you might have a problem with costs. You might be spending more for raw materials, or the salaries your company pays could be higher than normal industry levels.

Cost of goods sold

Reducing cost of goods sold may be a difficult in the short-term, especially if you're in a business where you have little or no control over the cost of raw materials. Another way to reduce costs is by studying and improving the manufacturing process. However, this usually takes several years and costs even more before real savings are reflected.

If you want to reduce waste in the production process, then you can implement LEAN initiatives by focusing on the actions that cost money but don't generate value for the company (or even destroy value):

- Reducing inventory (holding too much inventory increases carrying costs)

- Eliminating unnecessary movements of equipment or people
- Minimizing defects
- Reducing reprocessing and rework
- Analyzing unnecessary transportation
- Re-negotiating prices with providers
- Considering outsourcing
- Converting "fixed" into "variable" costs by paying per usage
- Unifying the assets your company is using (most airlines, for example, focus either on Boeing or Airbus as a provider for airplanes thus minimizing training and maintenance expenses)
- Simplifying the product or the service

General expenses

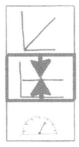

Reducing general expenses is much easier than reducing cost of goods sold, and can provide short-term benefits more quickly. In hard financial times, companies reduce expenses that aren't crucial (according to management) such as business trips, recruitment, and training. In some cases, a company will lay off employees.

Such actions have an immediate positive impact on the income statement and cash flow, but can reduce the company's long-term ability to generate value.

Options for cutting costs without harming the quality of the product or the work environment are limited, and it can be tempting to cross those lines for the sake of expediency. Management is accountable for the results of their initiatives should they continue to reduce expenses beyond a certain level.

Improve liquidity

Warning signs of cash flow problems include:
- Your company is constantly running out of cash and has to rely on expensive short-term financing such as factoring (selling its accounts receivable to a third party).
- You're unable to sell inventory in time when sales decline.
- You have accounts receivable past 60 days.

How can cash flow be improved?
- Re-examine and reduce your customers' credit terms. Charging more quickly will provide better liquidity and decrease your interest expenses, because you would need to borrow less.
- Improve billing. Submitting invoices sooner and following up with customers is usually effective.
- Reduce inventory.

Not using assets efficiently

Some challenges are not strictly financial but can negatively affect financial results. Lack of employee motivation can be considered an HR issue but if it escalates too far, talented people will start leaving the company. This HR issue, therefore, can increase expenses because of the need to recruit replacements, and could cause loss of revenue due to poor customer service.

Warning signs of such troubles include:
- Poor teamwork and lack of alignment between departments
- Projects not delivered on time or on budget
- Constant company re-organization
- Poor communication
- Increase of absenteeism
- Higher turnover

Create or destroy value: idea generator

Following, you will find a collection of over 30 strategies and how they affect:
- Sales
- Cost of goods sold/cost of service
- General expenses
- Use of assets
- Cash-flow

Purchasing new equipment as shown could help you reduce cost of goods sold because your production process will be more efficient. The same action, however, will be negative for your cash-flow (especially if you pay the total investment in cash). This purchase will also increase the general expenses. How will the new equipment affect profitability? Negatively in the short term, especially if it's a significant investment. In the long run, it could improve profitability because of the cumulative savings on expenses.

Keep in mind that in a complex system like a company, not all actions can be reduced to "black or white" and in some cases the result depends on many additional factors.

⚠ potential negative impact ✔ positive impact

	Sales	COGS	General Expenses	Profitability	Assets	Cash-flow
Have more stock	✔					⚠
Simplify			✔	✔	✔	
Reduce defects	✔			✔		
Reduce the need for transportation		✔				
Minimize waiting times					✔	✔
Reduce inventory	⚠				✔	✔
Promotion campaign	✔			⚠		✔
Produce more with the same capital		✔		✔	✔	
Reduce prices	⚠			⚠		✔
Produce less with the same capital		⚠		⚠	⚠	
Pay providers later						✔
Pay providers faster						⚠
Sell additional products or services	✔	⚠		✔	✔	
Offer just-in-time delivery	✔	⚠	⚠	⚠		⚠
Minimize waste		✔	✔	✔	✔	✔
Improve cost control	⚠	✔	✔	✔	✔	✔
Improve communication	✔	✔	✔	✔	✔	✔
Focus on more profitable customers	✔					
Focus on customers at the bottom of the	✔					⚠

pyramid						
Invest in R&D	✔		⚠			⚠
Eliminate unnecessary movement of people and equipment		✔		✔	✔	✔
Eliminate overproduction		✔	✔	✔	✔	✔
Delegate and empower	✔	✔	✔	✔	✔	✔
Buy raw materials in advance with a discount		✔				⚠
Charge faster		✔				✔
Learn from best practices	✔	✔	✔	✔	✔	✔
Save energy		✔	✔	✔	✔	
Green initiatives	✔	⚠	⚠			⚠
Sell on credit	✔			✔		⚠
Increase employees retention	✔	✔	✔	✔		
Improve employees recruitment			✔			✔
Use more external financing						✔
Use more internal financing						⚠
Pay salaries higher than industry norm	✔		⚠			⚠
Increase in advertising	✔		⚠			⚠
Raise prices	⚠			✔		⚠
Open new office (increase territory)	✔		✔			⚠

	Sell	COGS	General Expenses	Profitability	Assets	Cash-flow
Increase commissions for salespeople	✔	⚠		⚠		
Replace old equipment	✔	✔	⚠	⚠ ⚠	✔	⚠
Invest in customer service training	✔		⚠	✔		⚠
Invest in sales training	✔		⚠	✔		⚠
Teambuilding activities	✔	✔	⚠	✔		⚠

What other actions can you apply to your business? How will they affect sales, profitability, expenses, and cash-flow?

This page intentionally left blank.

Financial Crimes

How to detect and prevent fraud

"There was a small typing error in our Half-Year Results Statement. For 'profit', please read 'loss.'" Ex - CFO

Accounting fraud is a "white-collar" crime. Being able to detect such fraud helps you better protect your interests. Fraud can seriously harm the business itself as well as the stakeholders.
- Employees can lose their jobs, savings, and pension funds.
- Creditors and providers can suffer losses if they are unable to charge for their product or service.
- Shareholders could lose money because of the company's stock collapse.

Regulation has become more strict. The Sarbanes-Oxley Act was adopted for US public companies, and most countries have a similar equivalent. Even so, every year there are additional accounting scandals.

Fraud is difficult to uncover, especially because in most cases the auditor is also involved. In many examples scandals were exposed by internal whistle-blowers. In others, cheating became so evident that it could no longer be concealed.

In most circumstances, accounting fraud is deliberate. Below are some recent infamous examples:

- Increasing depreciation time for equipment (Waste Management, 1998)

- Keeping debt out of the balance sheet (Enron, 2001)
- Capitalizing rather than expensing costs (WorldCom, 2002)
- Inflating sales (Lehman Brothers, 2008)
- Manipulating stock price (AIG, 2005)

In others cases accounting scandals happen because of incompetent management.

In 2013, the French drug manufacturer Sanofi had a loss due to a huge write-off in Brazil. Expecting a future tax increase from the government, the company management began selling aggressively, assuming customers would buy now to save from the impending increase.

However, the product couldn't be sold due to the approaching expiration dates. The greater part of the inventory was returned to the company. The loss exceeded 122 million euros.

In another example, HP had to write off $8.8 billion due to the unsuccessful merger with Autonomy and having paid an "absurdly high" price despite many warnings. The write-off led to a dramatic loss in an otherwise stable company annual profit.

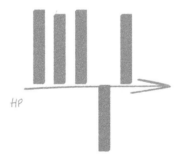

In the following pages you will find some common fraud techniques and how to detect them. Howe
ver, bear in mind that white-collar criminals become more and more creative.

Fake revenue

The company may record revenue that does not exist, especially when the end of the quarter or financial year is approaching. The goal here is to fake a growing demand for the company's services or product, something that usually increases the stock price.

Some indicators are:
- Channel stuffing. Sending inventory to distributors and recognizing it as a revenue long before the end customer buys it.
- Shipping goods that weren't even ordered
- Recognizing future sales in the current period. In the service industry, a delivery could last for several years. A common malpractice is to report it as a current sale instead of spreading it out according to the duration of the contract.
- Hold and bill. Recognizing a sale immediately after a buyer commits without actually shipping the goods.

How to detect it

- A regular sale should be converted into cash sooner or later. If revenue increases, so should cash flow. Also, a drastic rise in accounts receivable could mean that a company is recognizing sales that have not been made.
- A sudden growth in revenue could also be a sign, especially at the end of an accounting period. Perhaps this rise came from selling a primary asset, not a product or service. It's always advisable to compare the company's revenue growth with competitors. A sales increase that is much higher than competitors could be suspicious.
- The company's net profit margin is too high in comparison with the industry.
- The company has changed its revenue recognition policy as stated in the footnotes of its financial statement.

Hidden liabilities and expenses

Management can also "cook" its balance sheet by hiding liabilities. Examples include:
- Bad debt masked as accounts receivable
- Fixed assets that are obsolete, broken, or in need of repair
- Broken, expired, or obsolete inventory
- Pending lawsuits
- Environmental issues
- Tax liabilities

How to detect it

Some ways companies can distort liabilities or expenses:
- Instead of recognizing an expense, record it as an investment (capitalizing the expense). This action creates an asset that does not exist.
- Recognize short-term liability as long-term and create a false impression of better solvency.

Incorrect asset valuation

Just like hiding debt, recording fictitious assets makes the business look stronger and healthier.

Inventory is one of the easiest assets to manipulate because the volume is often overwhelming and because it's frequently distributed in different locations. The company could inflate the number of items, their value, or both. Such fraud can be difficult to discover without directly examining the physical inventory.

Fraud techniques include:
- Counting the same items repeatedly after moving them between different factories and warehouses
- Counting empty boxes as inventory
- "Borrowing" inventory from providers

Accounts receivable is another opportunity for manipulation. A company could record uncollectable debt as an asset.

In another example, a business could inflate the value of its fixed assets.

How to detect it

- Very low cost of goods sold when compared to revenue is a warning sign.
- Very slow inventory turnover compared to sales is also a red flag.
- Sales growth in accounts receivable instead of cash can indicate that a company is fabricating receivables.

Manipulate timing

One of the main principles of accounting (the matching principle) states that a company should report an expense during the revenue period in which it was generated.

Violating this principle and "playing" with the timing is often used to attempt fraud. Some common methods are:
- Recognizing future sales early, as mentioned before.
- Postponing expenses. A business could hold an invoice from a provider and not recognize it as an expense until the beginning of the next accounting period. This way, the profit for the current period looks higher.
- Paying expenses up front. If the management of a company is trying to sell it, they might absorb future costs in the current accounting period. As a result, the next period's profit will jump because costs were already absorbed.
- Depreciation. The company could also "play" with the terms of depreciation. Increasing the number of years over which an asset is depreciated will decrease the expenses in the income statement.
- To minimize taxes, the management could move expenses from one accounting period to another.

How to detect it

- Watch out for sudden sales growth at the end of the accounting period.
- Examine the terms of depreciation and whether they differ from the industry standards.
- Consider whether shipping costs are too low, as items recognized as a sale might not have been actually shipped to customers.

This page intentionally left blank.

Appendix 1: The one page model

This page intentionally left blank.

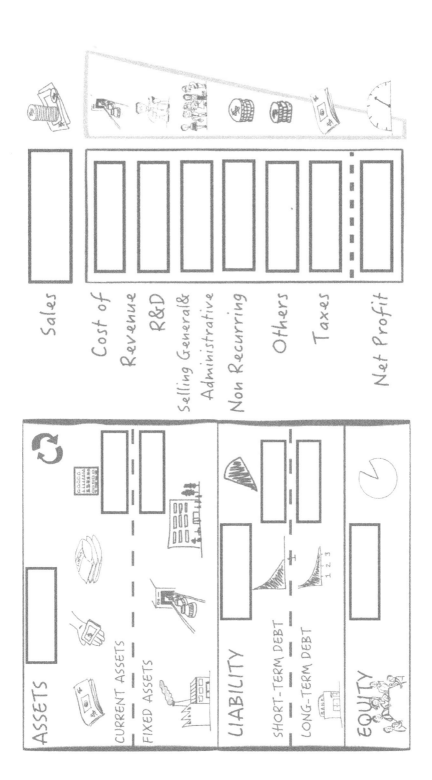

Sales

Cost of Revenue

R&D

Selling General & Administrative

Non Recurring

Others

Taxes

Net Profit

ASSETS

CURRENT ASSETS

FIXED ASSETS

LIABILITY

SHORT-TERM DEBT

LONG-TERM DEBT

EQUITY

153

This page intentionally left blank.

Appendix 2: Reading your company's financial report using the one page model

This page intentionally left blank.

Where and why to find it

Now let's take a look at your company's annual report and see how it can be decoded using what was already covered in this book.

If you work for a public company, then the company annual report can be easily downloaded from the company's website or portals such as Yahoo Finance.

If you work for a privately owned company, your management has no obligation to disclose an annual report, and they usually don't. However, there are companies that specialize in researching private businesses. Such services are Business Insights, Dun & Bradstreet, PrivCo, and ReferenceUSA. Business journals and branch organizations also publish financial information.

What is usually included in the annual report?
- An attractive title page
- Words from the management and summaries of the most relevant information
- Information about trends affecting the industry
- Future plans
- A list of current management
- A letter from auditors guaranteeing that the financial information represented has been audited and is truthful
- Financial statements including the balance sheet, income statement, cash flow statement, and variations in equity
- Many pages of fine print

What about the fine print?

One of the most astounding examples of the art of accounting is reducing a whole company to a one-page report, such as the income statement or the balance sheet.

Imagine a big multinational corporation with operations in several countries, selling to customers who use many currencies, and having to deal with different economic regulations. Totaling the value of all its assets into a single number takes an immense number of working hours and requires certain assumptions (estimations). This is one of the reasons financial teams are so stressed toward the end of the fiscal year.

The estimates are described in the fine print following a company report, which include information about:
- Depreciation methods. How long is the company using a piece of equipment? The shorter the period, the higher the annual depreciation expense well be.
- Uncollected receivables.
- Obsolete inventory.
- The probability of loss in litigation.

In addition to estimates, the fine print could also contain the following information:
- Notes on the financial statements. This is more detailed information about each row in the balance sheet and the income statement.
- Disclosure of the financial risks that the company has taken.

Resources

This page intentionally left blank.

Recommended internet resources

http://finance.yahoo.com
Easy-to-access financial reports and ratios for public companies, plus relevant economic news

http://www.gurufocus.com and http://www.csimarket.com
Accounting ratios by industry or company

http://www.wolframalpha.com
A knowledge search engine that can provide very useful financial information. (For example, "Apple Inc. revenue last 10 years")

http://www.financeformulas.net/Net_Present_Value.html
More information about how to calculate net present value

https://studies2.hec.fr/jahia/webdav/site/hec/shared/sites/jeanj ean/acces_eleves/finance%20a%20cour%20terme/Hggins.pdf
Information about calculating a company's growth equilibrium

Bibliography (sources for facts and statistics)

Markku Rimpiläinen. (2015). Sales and Marketing – More Important Than Ever. 2015, de Management Events Website: http://managementevents.com/news/sales-and-marketing-more-important-than-ever/

Wansink, Brian and Jeffrey Sobal (2007), "Mindless Eating: The 200 Daily Food Decisions We Overlook," Environment and Behavior 39:1, 106-123

Kulikova L.I., Goshunova A.V. (November 2014). Human Capital Accounting in Professional Sport: Evidence from Youth Professional Football. Mediterranean Journal of Social Sciences, Vol 5 No 24, 44-48.

Financial literacy surveys conducted by Atkinson et al., 2007, Fessler et al., 2007, Szafranska & Matysik-Pejas, 2010, Sibley, 2010, and O'Donnell & Keeney, 2009.

This page intentionally left blank.

Make the learning even more engaging

This page intentionally left blank.

Did you like the book and want to take it live with your team?

"How would your business change if every member of your organization acted like a business owner?"

 Silega **Pulse**™

Silega Pulse™ is a highly-customizable, powerful table-mat based business simulation. Participants manage all parts of the business process – planning, operations, finance, and personnel development. Teams make the kinds of decisions made by actual business owners: how to price products, which customers and markets to compete for, how much stock to buy, and how to pay suppliers. At the same time, participants have the opportunity to see what the other departments and organizational functions are experiencing all along.

Short analysis sessions are conducted after each period of activity, followed by immediate application exercises.

This simulation can be adapted for different business types (retail, manufacturing, etc.) and can even be personalized to include numbers from your company's balance sheets.

Please visit our website for more information.
http://www.silega.com/pulse

This page intentionally left blank.

About the Author

Georgi Tsvetanov

Email: georgi.tsvetanov@silega.com
LinkedIn Profile ca.linkedin.com/in/georgi

Regional Director for Silega Americas since 2010, Georgi has worked in the Training & Development field for over ten years for global customers within the FMCG, pharmaceutical, banks and financial, manufacturing, and retail industries. He studied Economics at the University of National and World Economy in Sofia, and also has a Bachelor's degree in Human Resources Management with specialization in Training and Coaching from the Person Technological University of Latin America.

Mr. Tsvetanov has facilitated more than 450 experiential learning sessions (some with up to 500 simultaneous participants) in countries including the U.S.A, Mexico, China, Singapore, Indonesia, Malaysia, Brazil, Argentina, Turkey, Colombia, Dubai, Ecuador, Dominican Republic, Romania, Guatemala, and Spain.

He is also a frequent speaker at the largest training and development conference, ATD (previously ASTD) International Conference & Exhibition and the ABSEL (Association for Business Simulation and Experiential Learning) Annual Conference.

This page intentionally left blank.

Special Thanks

This book would have been impossible without a handful of people. Personal thanks to Silega's global team, distributors, and the thousands of participants in the Pulse simulation workshops around the world.

Special credits to Kalin Blajev for the help and advice.

Printed in the USA
CPSIA information can be obtained
at www.ICGtesting.com
LVHW020411141123
763881LV00004B/267